STUDIES IN SOCIALISM

SOCIALIST CLASSICS

Available from Spokesman

A History of British Socialism
Max Beer

Cromwell and Communism
Eduard Bernstein

The Levellers and the English Revolution
H. N. Brailsford

Readings and Witnesses for Workers' Control
Ken Coates & Tony Topham

A Radical Reader
Christopher Hampton

Social and Economic Writings
Tom Mann

Roads to Freedom
Bertrand Russell

Pig's Meat
Thomas Spence

The Attack
R. H. Tawney

The Industrial Syndicalist 1910-1911

The Syndicalist 1912-1914

Studies in Socialism

by
Jean Jaurès

Introduced by
J. E. Mortimer
Leon Trotsky
J. Ramsay MacDonald

SPOKESMAN

Translated by Mildred Minturn

First published in 1906
This edition published in 2008 by
Spokesman
Russell House
Bulwell Lane, Nottingham NG6 0BT, England
Phone 0115 9708318
Fax 0115 9420433
e-mail elfeuro@compuserve.com
www.spokesmanbooks.com

ISBN13: 978 0 85124 749 6

New introduction copyright J. E. Mortimer 2008

A CIP Catalogue record is available from the British Library

Printed by the Russell Press Ltd
(phone 0115 9784505 www.russellpress.com)

Contents

FOREWORD TO 2008 EDITION *by J.E.Mortimer*   vii

JAURÈS *by Leon Trotsky*   x

EDITOR'S NOTE *by J. Ramsay MacDonald*   xiv

SOCIALISM –
The Socialist Aim   1
Socialism and Life   9
The Radicals and Private Property   22
Socialism and the Privileged Classes   34

THE PROBLEM OF METHOD –
The Problem of Socialist Method   40
Some Sayings of Liebknecht   81
Liebknecht on Socialist Tactics   90
"To Expand, not to Contract"   98
Revolutionary Evolution   105
Revolutionary Majorities   113
Necessity for a Majority   122
General Strike and Revolution   135

SPEECH AT THE ANGLO-FRENCH PARLIAMENTARY DINNER   159

MOONLIGHT   165

struggle for the rights of human beings embodied in declarations associated with the French Revolution. Jaurès inherited the spirit of the radical wing of the French Revolution and this influenced his approach to human freedom in the struggle for socialism.

The third essay (pages 22 to 33) provides a telling commentary on the concept of private property. Only under socialism, Jaurès asserts, will it be possible to ensure that 'no man will be able to make use of other men to create dividends for himself, or profit, or an income, or rent'.

The fourth essay (pages 34 to 39) expresses the essential humanitarianism of Jaurès. He wants to 'free the great work of proletarian revolution from the sickening and cruel odour of blood, of murder and of hate which still clings to the bourgeois revolution'. The quotation reminds one of the speech and revelations of Khrushchev at the 20th Congress of the Communist Party of the Soviet Union (CPSU). On the other hand, Jaurès did not live through the experience of fascism and the Second World War. There is, however, a vital difference between the conduct of fascism and the conduct of controversy on the road to socialism. Humanitarianism is an important ingredient of socialist conduct.

The succeeding eight essays (pages 40 to 158) in the book are all addressed to the central problem of the method of the transition to socialism.

Jaurès argues that the proletariat is growing in numbers, in solidarity and in self-consciousness. This is probably still true on a world scale, but in some of the economically advanced countries, notably the United States, Britain and Germany, the traditional proletariat associated with heavy industry has now declined in number. It has, however, been accompanied by an expansion in the number of non-industrial employees including, for example, supermarket assistants, call-centre workers, health service and other social workers, teachers at all levels, and technicians over a wide range of services and industries. Some of these groups, particularly in the private sector, have shown less readiness to organise in trade unions than the traditional industrial working class. This problem has still to be resolved.

Jaurès links the growth of the proletariat with the realisation of socialism (page 44), and argues that the means of victory will be through universal suffrage, trade unions, co-operative societies, and various branches of 'public service in the democratic state' (pages 45 and 46). It is at this stage that Jaurès questions the seizure of power by revolution.

Marx and Engels, according to Jaurès, saw the possibility of proletarian

Foreword to 2008 Edition

Studies in Socialism by Jean Jaurès was first published by the Independent Labour Party (ILP) in 1906. It consists of a number of essays, most of them centred on the method of transition from capitalism to socialism in the economically advanced countries.

The special point of these essays is that they reaffirm very vigorously the essential features of the analysis of capitalism made by Marx and Engels. They also illustrate the influence on Jaurès of the traditions of the French Revolution (and particularly the radical wing represented by Babeuf). Nevertheless, the essays challenge the interpretation sometimes made by Marxists about the method of transition from capitalism to socialism. The essays affirm strongly the case for democratic endeavour by socialists in seeking to change society.

These essays were, of course, written before the two World Wars and the experience of fascism. I feel sure that if Jean Jaurès had lived through the World Wars and fascism, he would have taken account of them in his conclusions. It was Jefferson who spoke of the right of revolution for citizens who are denied the opportunity of peaceful change. I think it likely that Jaurès would have applied Jefferson's logic to the struggle against fascism and the conduct of unjust wars.

The strong argument of Jaurès for a commitment to democratic action in the transition to socialism has relevance to the experience of the Soviet Union and a number of Eastern European countries. His enthusiasm for the potentiality of universal suffrage in the struggle for socialism reminds me also of the sentiments expressed by Engels in his revised introduction to Marx's *The Class Struggles in France 1848-50*. He wrote the revised introduction in 1895, shortly before his death. This essay of Engels was distorted by some Social-Democrat leaders to imply that Engels rejected revolutionary action in all circumstances. This was not so, but it was true that Engels expressed enthusiasm for the electoral progress made by the German Social Democratic Party. He wrote that the bourgeoisie 'can be much more afraid of the legal than of the illegal action of the workers' party, of the results of elections than of those of rebellion'.

The first essay (pages 1 to 8) is relatively short, but it is a forceful explanation of the case for socialism, with an emphasis on the relevance of the nation state for the framework of the struggle.

The second essay (pages 9 to 21) is an assertion of the continuing forgotten comes to life and the dead men rise up again. And traditions reveal all of their might. Where are they hiding? In the mysterious reservoirs of the unconscious somewhere at the extremities of the nerves that have undergone a historical processing which no decree can now repeal or abolish. Thus out of 1793 grew 1830, 1848 and 1871.

Imponderable and ethereal as these traditions are, they are however now becoming a real factor in politics for they are capable of becoming incarnate. Even in the worst days of its fallen spirit the French proletariat, torn to pieces in factions and sects, stood like a warning shadow over the official leaders of the fatherland. That is why the immediate political influence of the French workers has always been higher than their level of organization and their parliamentary representation. And it is in this historical force, which goes on from generation to generation, that Jaurès is strong.

But this Jaurès, the bearer of a heritage, is still not the whole Jaurès. He presents another side towards us, that of a parliamentarian of the Third Republic. A parliamentarian from top to toe! His world is that of the electoral pact, the parliamentary platform, the challenging question, the oratorical duel, the backstage agreement and, at times, the ambiguous compromise ... A compromise against which traditions and objectives alike – the past and the future – might be quick to protest. Where is the psychological knot which ties these two faces together?

'The practical man,' says Renan in his article on Cousin, 'has to be base. If he has lofty goals they will only mislead him. It is for this reason that great people take part in practical life only through their shortcomings and petty qualities.' In these words of a contemplative sceptic and spiritual Epicurean it is not hard to find they key to Jaurès contradictions: assuming that here we have not a malicious slander on man in general but on Jaurès in particular. All of life is practice, creation and doing. 'Lofty goals' cannot mislead for they are merely its organs, and practice will always maintain its supreme control over them. To say that practical man, i.e. *social man*, must be for the most part base means simply to expose one's own moral cynicism, to fear its practical conclusions and to immerse oneself in idealistic speculations.

Jaurès destroys Renan's slander on man by his whole moral stature. An impatient active idealism guides him in even his most foolhardy moves.

In the darkest days of Millerandism – 1902 – I had occasion to see Jaurès next to Millerand on the platform, hand in hand, apparently linked in a complete unity of aims and resource. But an unmistakable feeling told me that an unbridgeable abyss separated them: this extreme enthusiast, selfless and ardent, from that parliamentary careerist, cold and calculating. There is something overwhelmingly convincing, a sort of infantile athletic sincerity in his figure, his voice and his gestures ...

On the platform he seems huge and yet he is below average height. Thick-set, with a head sitting squarely on his neck, with expressive 'dancing' cheekbones, nostrils which swell up as he speaks wholly releasing the stream of his passion, he in appearance too belongs to the same human type as Mirabeau and Danton. As an orator he is incomparable and has met no comparison. There is not that finished and at time irritating refinement in his speech with which Vandervelde shines. He cannot be compared with Bebel for a logical force of attraction. The cruel and venomous irony of Victor Adler is foreign to him. But in spirit, in passion and in his verve he is the equal of them all ...

It is true that another thoroughbred Russian discovered in Jaurès merely a skilful technical erudition and pseudo-classical declamation. But what speaks in such an appraisal is nothing more than the poverty of our native culture. The French have an oratorical technique, a common heritage which they adopt without effort, and outside of which they are as inconceivable as a 'respectable' man without formal dress. Every speaking Frenchman speaks well. Hence the harder it is for a Frenchman to be a great orator. But Jaurès was just such. It is not his rich technique nor his enormous miraculous sounding voice nor the generous profuseness of his gestures but the *genius's naïveté of his enthusiasm* which brings Jaurès close to the masses and makes him what he is ...

But we have digressed from our question: what is the psychological knot which ties up in Jaurès an inheritor of Promethean traditions with a parliamentary operator?

What is Jaurès? An opportunist? Or a revolutionary? Both the one and the other depending on the political moment; and moreover he is ready to go to the ultimate extremes in either direction. Jaurès is a figure of *action*. He is always prepared to 'crown the thought with the crown of execution' ... During the Dreyfus Case Jaurès said to himself: 'whoever does not seize the executioner's hand poised over his victim will himself become the executioner's accomplice', and without pondering the political outcome of the campaign he threw himself into the flood of Dreyfusism. His teacher, friend and subsequent irreconcilable antagonist, Guesde, told him: 'Jaurès, I like you because your deed always follows on your thought!'

Herein lies the strength and the weakness of Jaurès.

'Any age believes,' wrote Heine, 'that its own struggle is more important than that of all the rest. It is in this that the faith of an age consists and it is in this faith that it lives and dies ...'

In Jaurès there is something beyond this religion of his age: he has the élan of the *moment*. He does not measure the transient political alignments against the great yardstick of historical perspectives. He is wholly and completely here amid the evil of the hour. And in serving the hour he is not afraid of coming into conflict with his higher aim. He expends his passion, energy and talent with such a spontaneous extravagance as if the outcome of the great struggle of the two worlds depended on each political question taken one by one.

In this strength of Jaurés lies, too, his fatal weakness. His politics lack proportion and frequently he cannot see the wood for the trees.

There is a tide in the affairs of men (says Shakespeare's Brutus)
Which, taken at the flood, leads on to fortune;
Omitted, all the voyage of their life
Is bound in shallows and in miseries.

In the mould and the scale of his character Jaurès was born for the epoch of the great flood. But he was fated to develop his talent in the period of grave European reaction. This is not his fault but his misfortune. But this misfortune in turn engendered his fault. Among his gifts Jaurès lacks one: the ability to *wait*. Not to wait sitting idly by, but to gather one's forces and prepare the tackle confidently reckoning on the approaching tempest. He wants immediately to switch over to the jangling coinage of practical success, to the great traditions and the great opportunities. From there he falls so often into insoluble contradictions 'in shallows and in miseries' of the Third Republic ...

Only a blind man would number Jaurès among the doctrinaires of political compromise. To such politics he has merely added his talents, his passion and his ability to go through to the end but he has not made a catechism out of it. And in the event Jairès will be the first to unfurl his mainsail and move off the shallows out to the open sea ...

Leon Trotsky
Kievskaya Mysl No. 9, 9 January 1909

Editor's Note

The papers included in this volume are particularly important at the present moment, because they discuss the question of Socialist methods under Parliamentary government. Whilst a Socialist party in a country is so rudimentary that it has no influential representation on administrative or legislative authorities, it grows by the revolutionary method of isolation; it prides itself in its moments of defeat in the fact that at any rate it shouted Socialism often enough and loud enough, and that the votes it received were those of convinced Socialists. The Socialist movements in France, Germany, and Belgium have gone far beyond that stage. In Germany, owing to the fact that the Reichstag is not the Parliament of a democratically governed people, the Parliamentary successes of Socialism have not forced it to adapt itself to the Parliamentary method of organic change, and the German Socialist still sees the fiery spirit of Revolution as the companion of the angel which symbolises the spirit of his Socialist faith. But even in Germany, when the second ballots are held, the Socialist in practice ceases to declare that there is nothing in the State but one bourgeois and one Socialist party, for he then discriminates between the various sections of the bourgeois party and supports that which is most favourable to himself. Not only is this also the case in Belgium and in France, but the election of a Radical majority in the former country would probably lead to the inclusion of Socialists in the Ministry; whilst in France, at a time of great danger to the Republic, the most important section of the Socialists determined to support one of their comrades as a Minister. Whatever awkwardness may have resulted in M. Millerand's actions as a member of a Cabinet, this vital point in Socialist method will not be decided by a solitary experiment. No Socialist, however, could enter a Cabinet, whilst retaining his membership of a Socialist organisation, except with the consent of his Party.

At last Great Britain has its Socialist and Labour Party in Parliament, and it is of the utmost moment that British Socialists should study Continental Socialist methods first hand. The main stream of British Socialism has been too long isolated from the Continental movement, and that movement has been presented to us through reddened spectacles. Readers of the following papers will discover how little sympathy the most powerful figure amongst French Socialists has with much that has been written in this country on what the proper Socialist method should be.

A Parliamentary Socialist Party may adopt one of three methods. It may content itself with permeating other parties, in which case it is purely educational and never can secure guarantees that its work is to be permanent; it may be an isolated factor, in which case it must remain revolutionary and impotent except as a spur to other parties; it may be independent merely, in which case it can combine the educational value of the permeation method and the enthusiasm of the revolutionary method, and yet by the strength of its separate organisation secure a guarantee that every change in opinion and legislation is but the prelude to an ampler change, and by its authority in administrative and legislative bodies effect such fundamental readjustments in Social organisation as are entitled to be described as revolutionary. Since the beginning of the Independent Labour Party, this last has been the distinctive method of the great bulk of the organised Socialists in this country, and the success of the Labour Party at the recent elections necessitates a further development of the method—on the lines of these essays, it seems to me.

We are beholding in this country today Socialism moving from the forum into the senate. Upon that change, many others must follow. For instance, the irresponsible Socialism of the forum is a state of society conceived as something apart from the present state, an ideal built up anew from rational economics and conceptions of justice; whilst the Socialism of the senate is the co-ordination into a system, of numerous tendencies in present-day society every one of which has to work itself out and has to find expression in many different directions. The Socialist in authority is an evolutionist; he is as conscious of the actual movement towards his goal as of that goal itself; he is therefore as much concerned with wise methods as with just principles. He does not separate them but considers them both essential to his work as a Socialist. In consequence of this, he is faced with a new task, which, for a time, his old propagandist attitude of mind somewhat handicaps him in carrying out. He has to select from many contemporary tendencies those making for Socialism; he has to bring those tendencies into sympathetic touch and quicken them into a consciousness of their complete and common end; he has to create a Socialistic movement to give backing to his Socialist policy; his work is completed when he has created a party moved by the Socialist spirit and embracing the Socialist tendencies of his times. To him

Socialism is not a state but a guiding idea. For a Socialist candidate, therefore, to pride himself that he has only received Socialist votes, or for a Socialist elector to resolve on principle to vote only for Socialist candidates, is to show that he is only in the propagandist, the revolutionary, the statical stage of the movement, when everything is embryonic, before the movement has gained any authority. So soon as the Socialist is put in a position which enables him to play a part as administrator or legislator, he must not only push out towards the Socialist state, but he must also keep the road clear to that state. He is like a man getting through a somewhat turbulent crowd. He must occasionally discuss with the crowd its own interests, he must occasionally side with some faction, but all the time he is trying to get home.

The emphasis here placed upon method must not be misunderstood. Method and tactics are the most barren devices when pursued alone. The manipulation of party, the balancing of numbers, the bargaining and threatening for an advantageous position, when employed as an important means to a great end will be found to be futile. Opinion and conviction are ultimately the only foundations for permanent political and social change, and the Socialist must always remember that an understanding of and a sympathy with his general principles and his view of the relation between the community and the individual, are essential to the success of his social experiments whether administrative or legislative. What is here offered is not, therefore, merely a treatise in manipulation, but one in the nature of the forces that are making for Socialism and their organisation by a Socialist political party. A study of these essays will disabuse the minds of many British Socialists of mistaken ideas regarding Continental Socialist policy, and will impart to our British method of independence a fulness and an elasticity which it has not yet acquired.

J. Ramsay MacDonald
1906

STUDIES IN SOCIALISM.

THE SOCIALIST AIM.

THE first condition of success for Socialism is that its essential characteristics should be explained clearly, so that everyone can understand them. There are many misunderstandings created by our adversaries, and some created by ourselves. We must do away with these.

The main idea of Socialism is simple and noble. The Socialists believe that the present form of property holding divides Society into two great classes. One of these classes, the wage earning, the Proletariat, is obliged to pay to the other, the Capitalist, a sort of tax, in order to be able to live at all, and exercise its faculties to any degree. Here is a multitude of human beings, citizens; they possess nothing, they can live only by their work. But in order to work they need an expensive equipment which they have not got, and raw materials and capital which they have not got. Another class owns the means of production, the land, the factories, the machines, the raw materials, and accumulated capital in the form of money, and naturally this capitalist and possessing class, taking advantage of its power, makes the working and non-owning class pay a large forfeit. It does not rest content after it has been reimbursed for the advances it made and has repaired the wear and tear of the machinery. It levies in addition every year and indefinitely a considerable tax on the product of the workman and farmer, in the form of rent for farms, ground rent, rent of land in the cities, taxes for the payment of the public debt, industrial profit, commercial profit, and interest on stocks and bonds.

Therefore, in our present society, the work of the workers is not their exclusive property. And since, in our society founded on intensive production, economic activity is an essential function of every human being, as work forms an integral part of personality, the proletarian does not own his own body absolutely. The proletarian alienates a part of his activity, that is, a part of his being, for the profit of another class. The rights of man are incomplete and mutilated in him. He cannot perform a single act of his life without submitting to this restriction of his rights, this alienation of his very individuality. He has hardly left the factory, the mine, or the yard, where part of his effort has been expended in the creation of dividends and profits for the benefit of Capital, he has hardly gone back to the poor tenement where his family is huddled together, when he is face to face with another tax, other dues in the shape of rent. And besides this, State taxation in all its forms, direct taxation and indirect taxation, pares down his already twice diminished wage, and this not only to provide for the legitimate running expenses of a civilised society and for the advantage of all its members, but to guarantee the crushing payment of interest on the public debt for the profit of that same capitalist class, or for the maintenance of armaments at once formidable and useless. When, finally, the proletarian trys to buy, with the remnant of wages left to him after these inroads, the commodities which are necessities of daily life, he has two courses open to him. If he lacks time or money, he will turn to a retail dealer, and will then have to bear the expense of a cumbrous and unnecessary organisation of intermediary agents ; or else he may go to a great store, where over and above the direct expenses of management and distribution he has to provide for the profit of ten or twelve per cent. on the capital invested. Just as the old feudal road was blocked and cut up at every step by toll-rights and dues, so, for the proletarian the road of life is cut by the feudal rights imposed upon him by Capital. He can neither work nor eat, clothe nor shelter himself without paying a sort of ransom to the owning and capitalist class.

And not only his life but his very liberty suffers by this system. If labor is to be really free, all the workers should be called upon to take part in the management of the work. They should have a share in the economic government of the shop, just as universal suffrage gives them a share in the political government of the city. Now, in the capitalist organisation of labor, the laborers play a passive role. They neither decide, nor do they help in deciding, what work shall be done nor in what direction available energies shall be employed. Without their consent, and often even without their knowledge, the capital which they have created undertakes or abandons this or that enterprise. They are the "hands" of the capitalist system, only required to put into execution the schemes that capital alone has decided on. And the proletariat accomplishes these enterprises planned and willed by capital under the direction of chiefs selected by capital. So that the workers neither co-operate in determining the object of the work nor in regulating the mechanism of authority under which the work is performed. In other words, labor is doubly enslaved, since it is directed toward ends which it has not willed by means which it has not chosen. And so the same capitalist system which exploits the labor power of the workman restricts the liberty of the laborer. Thus the personality of the proletarian is lessened as well as his substance.

But this is not all. The capitalist and owning class is only a class apart when considered in relation to the wage-earners. It is itself divided and torn by the bitterest competition. It has never been able to organise itself, and in so doing to control production, and regulate it according to the variable needs of society. In this state of anarchical disorder, capital is only warned of its mistakes through crises, the terrible consequences of which often fall upon the proletariat, so, by the extreme of injustice, the working-classes are socially responsible for the carrying on of production, which they have no share in regulating.

To have responsibility without authority, to be punished without being even consulted—such is the paradoxical fate of the proletariat under the capitalist disorder. And if capital were organised, if by means of vast trusts it were able to regulate production, it would only regulate it for its own profit. It would abuse the power gained by union to impose usurious prices on the community of buyers, and the working-class would escape from economic disorder only to fall under the yoke of monopoly.

All this misery, all this injustice and disorder, result from the fact that one class monopolizes the means of production and of life, and imposes its law on another class, and on society as a whole. The thing to do, therefore, is to break down this supremacy of one class. The oppressed class must be enfranchised, and with it the whole of society. All difference of class must be abolished by transferring to the whole body of citizens—the organised community, the ownership of the means of production and of life, which to-day, in the hands of a single class, is a power of exploitation and oppression. The universal co-operation of all citizens must be substituted for the disorderly and abusive rule of the minority. This is the only method by which the individual can be enfranchised. And that is why the essential aim of Socialism, whether Collectivist or Communist, is to transform capitalist property into social property.

In the present state of humanity, where our only organisation is on the basis of nationality, social property will take the form of national property. But the action of the proletariat will assume more and more an international character. The various nations which are evolving towards Socialism will regulate their dealings with each other more and more according to the principles of justice and peace. But for a long time to come the nation as such will furnish the historical setting of Socialism; it will be the mould in which the new justice will be cast.

Let no one be astonished that we bring forward the idea of a national community now, whereas at first we set ourselves to establish the liberty of individuals. The nation, and the nation alone, can enfranchise all the citizens. Only the nation can furnish the means of free development to all. Private associations, temporary and limited in character, can protect limited groups of individuals only for a time. But there is only one universal association that can guarantee the rights of all individuals without exception, not only the rights of the living, but of those who are yet unborn, and who will take their places in the generations to come.

Now this universal and imperishable association, which includes all the individuals on a particular portion of the planet, and which extends its action and its thought to successive generations, is the nation. If, then, we invoke the nation, we do so in order to insure the rights of the individual in the fullest and most universal sense. Not a single human being for a single moment of time should be excluded from the sphere of rights. Not one should be in danger of becoming the prey or the instrument of another individual. Not one should be deprived of the sure means of laboring freely without servile dependence on any other individual.

In the nation, therefore, the rights of all

individuals are guaranteed, to-day, to-morrow, and for ever. If we transfer what was once the property of the capitalist class to the national community, we do not do this to make an idol of the nation, or to sacrifice to it the liberty of the individual. No, we do it that the nation may serve as a common basis for all individual activities and rights. Social rights, national rights, are only the geometric locus of the rights of all individuals.

Social ownership of property is merely opportunity of action brought within the reach of all.

SOCIALISM AND LIFE.

THE domination of one class is an attempt to degrade humanity. Socialism, which will abolish all primacy of class, and indeed all class, restores humanity to its highest level. It is therefore a duty for all men to be Socialists.

Let no one object, as do some Socialists and Positivists, that it is useless and childish to invoke justice, that justice is a metaphysical conception, susceptible of being twisted in any direction, and that all tyrannies have fashioned a cloak for themselves from this same worn-out purple. No, in modern society the word justice is taking on an ever larger and more definite meaning. It has come to signify that in every man, in every individual, humanity ought to be fully respected and exalted to its complete stature. Now, true humanity can only exist where there is independence, active exercise of the will, free and joyous adaptation of the individual to the whole. Where men are dependent on the favour of others, where individual wills do not co-operate freely in the work of society, where the individual submits to the law of the whole under compulsion or by force of habit, and not from reason alone, there humanity is degraded and mutilated. It is, therefore, only by the abolition of the reign of Capital and the establishment of Socialism that humanity can come into the fulness of its heritage.

I am perfectly aware that the revolutionary bourgeoisie managed to infuse an oligarchical tone, the spirit of a single class, into the Declaration of the Rights of Man. I am aware that it tried to embody in that Declaration, and so consecrate for ever, the bourgeois forms of property-holding, and that even in the political world it began by refusing the right of suffrage to millions of the poor, who would thus have become passive citizens. But I know also that the democrats immediately made use of the theory of the Rights of Man, of all men, to demand and to conquer the right of suffrage for all. I know that they immediately based even their economic demands on that same theory. I know that the working-class, although in 1789 its existence as a self-conscious class was only rudimentary, did not hesitate to apply and to enlarge the Rights of Man in a proletarian direction. After 1792 it proclaimed that the ownership of life is the foremost of all our possessions and that the right over this sovereign property should have precedence of all the others. Now let this word "life" be boldly expanded: let its meaning comprise not bare subsistence only, but all life, all the development of human faculties, and it will appear that Communism itself was grafted by the proletariat on to the Declaration of the Rights of Man. Thus the human rights proclaimed by the Revolution instantly took on a vaster and deeper meaning than that given to it by the revolutionary bourgeoisie. That class was the upholder of rights still too oligarchical and restricted to cover the whole sphere of human rights: the bed of the river was larger than the river, and a new stream, the great proletarian and human flood, had to join it before the idea of justice could be fulfilled at last.

Socialism alone can give its true meaning to the Declaration of the Rights of Man and realize the whole idea of human justice. The justice of the revolutionary bourgeoisie has freed humanity from many personal fetters: but in forcing each new generation to pay a tax to the capital accumulated by the generations that have preceded it, and in leaving to the minority the privilege of collecting this tax, it has in a sense mortgaged the personality of every living human being for the benefit of the past and of a single class.

We, on the contrary, maintain that the means of production and wealth accumulated by humanity should be at the disposal of human activity in all its forms and should free them. According to us, every man has henceforth a right to the means of development which society has created. It is not then a human being, in all his weakness and nakedness, that is born into the world, exposed to every form of oppression and exploitation. It is a person invested with a right, who can claim for his perfect development the free use of the means of labour that have been accumulated by human effort.

Every human being has a right to complete growth. He has then the right to exact from humanity everything which can supplement his own effort. He has the right to work, to produce, and to create, and no class of men should be able to exact usury from the fruit of his work and bring it under their yoke. And as the community can only ensure the rights of the individual by putting the means of production at his disposal, the community itself must have the sovereign right of ownership over all the means of production.

Marx and Engels have brought out magnificently in the Communist Manifesto that respect for all life which is the very essence of Communism. "In bourgeois society living labour is only a means of adding to labour which has been accumulated in the form of capital. In Communist Society, accumulated labour will be only a means of enlarging, enriching and stimulating the life of the labourers.

"In bourgeois society the past dominates the present. In Communist Society, the present will dominate the past."

The Declaration of the Rights of Man had also been an affirmation of life, a call to life. The Revolution proclaimed the rights of the living man. It did not recognize the right of past humanity to bind present humanity. It did not recognize in the past services of kings and nobles the right to bear heavily on the present living humanity and stop its growth. On the contrary, the living humanity seized hold of and appropriated to its own use all that was vital and strong in the legacy of the past.

The unity of France, which had been the work of royalty, became the decisive instrument of revolution against royalty itself. In the same way the great forces of production amassed by the bourgeoisie will become the decisive instrument of human liberation from the power of capitalist privilege.

Life does not destroy the past : it subdues it to its own ends. The Revolution is not a rupture ; it is a conquest. And when the proletariat has conquered, when Communism has been instituted, all the stored up human effort of centuries will become a sort of supplementary nature, rich and beneficent, which will welcome all human beings from the hour of their birth, and assure to them their full development.

. . . .

The roots of Communism, then, strike far back, even to the bourgeois conception of justice, to the Declaration of the Rights of Man and the right to life. But this internal logic of the idea of right and humanity would have remained dormant and powerless without the external vigorous action of the proletariat. The proletariat intervened from the very first days of the Revolution. It did not listen to the absurd advice given by those who, like Marat, animated by the spirit of class, said: "What are you doing? Why are you going to seize the Bastille, whose walls never imprisoned a working-man?" It marched to the attack, determined the success of great victories, rushed to the frontier, saved the Revolution at home and abroad, became an indispensable power, and gathered as it went the fruits of its incessant activity. In three years, from 1789 to 1792, it transformed a semi-democratic and semi-middle-class system to a pure democracy, in which proletarian action was sometimes even the dominant factor. Having shown the strength of which it was capable, it gained self confidence, and ended by telling itself, with Babeuf, that the new power it had created, the national power that was the common possession of all, ought to be made the instrument by whose means happiness for all could be established.

Thus, by the action of the proletariat, Communism ceased to be a vague philosophic speculation and became a party, a living force. Thus, Socialism arose from the French Revolution under the combined action of two forces, the force of the idea of right and the force of the new-born activity of the proletariat. It is, therefore, not a Utopian abstraction. It gushes forth from the most turbulent and effervescent of the hot springs of modern life.

But now, after many tests, half victories and repulses, through the diversities of political régimes, the new middle-class order developed. Now, under the Empire and the Restoration, the economic system of the bourgeoisie, based on unlimited competition, began to bear its fruit: undoubted increase of wealth, but with it immorality, trickery, perpetual warfare, disorder and oppression. Fourier's stroke of genius was to conceive that it was possible to remedy the confusion, to purge and organise the social system without hampering the production of wealth, but on the contrary, increasing it. His was no ascetic ideal. He wished for free play for all faculties, for all instincts. The same association that would abolish crises would multiply riches by regulating and combining all effort. Thus the slight cloud of asceticism that may have overshadowed Socialism was dispelled. Thus, Socialism, having taken part with the proletarians of the Revolution, and with Babeuf, in all the revolutionary life, came finally into the great current of modern wealth and production. As represented by Fourier and St.

Simon it appears at last as a power able not only to overcome capitalism, but to surpass it in its own field.

In the new order foreseen by these great geniuses, justice will not be obtained at the price of the joys of life; on the contrary, the just organisation of human forces will add to their productive power. The splendour of wealth will be a manifestation of the triumph of right, and happiness will be the halo of justice. Babeufism was not the negation of the Revolution, but, on the contrary, its hardiest pulsation. So Fourierism and Saint-Simonism are not the negation, the restriction of modern life, but its passionate increase. Everywhere then, Socialism is a vital force, moving in the direction of life itself, and in its fiercest current.

But the reply of the bourgeoisie under Louis Philippe to the great visions of harmony and wealth for all, the vast constructive conceptions of Fourier and Saint Simon, was a redoubled fury of class exploitation by the exhaustive intensive use made of the labour element in production, and an orgy of State concessions, monopolies, dividends and premiums. It would have been naïve, to say the least, to continue to oppose idyllic dreams to this shameless exploitation. The retort of Proudhon was a biting criticism of property, interest, rent of farms and profit: and here again the word which ought to have been spoken, was uttered under the very dictation, the sharp inspiration of life itself.

But how was the work of criticism to be completed by the work of organisation? How were all the social elements that were threatened or oppressed by the power of capital, the banks, and industrial monopoly, to be united in one fighting whole? Proudhon quickly discovered that the army of social democracy was composed of very various elements; that it was a mixture of factory-workers, still weak in numbers and power, of a lower middle-class composed of petty manufacturers and small tradespeople, and of an artisan class which the absorbing power of capital was eyeing greedily, but had not yet absorbed.

From this analysis comes all that is hazy and contradictory in the positive constructive part of Proudhon's work, that singular mixture of reaction and revolution which makes him endeavour on the one hand to save the lower middle-class by means of artificial combinations of credit, and, on the other, urge the creation of a solid working-class, the revolutionary power. He seems to have wished to suspend the action of events, to put off the revolutionary crisis of 1848, in order to give economic evolution time to draw its line of action more clearly, and to direct the minds of men better. But here again, whence come these hesitations, these scruples, even the contradictory nature of these efforts, if not from the influence of the intimate contact of sincere Socialist thought with the complex and still uncertain reality. It is the very life of modern times that again and again finds its echo here.

And now at last, after 1848, the prime effective force behind the whole movement has become organised ; now, everyone can understand and realise it. Now the growth of modern industry has brought forth a working proletariat, increasingly numerous, coherent, and self-conscious. Those who with Marx hailed the advent of this decisive power, those who have understood that the world was to be transformed by its means, have perhaps shown a tendency to exaggerate the rapidity of economic evolution. Less prudent than Proudhon, and not allowing as he did for the power of resistance and resources of self-transformation in the class of small producers, they have perhaps over-simplified the problem and magnified the absorbing faculty of concentrated capital.

But even after we have made all the reservations and restrictions which result from the study of the complicated and many-sided reality, the truth remains that the proletariat is increasing in number, that it represents an ever-growing fraction of human societies, and that it is gathered together in always vaster centres of production ; the truth remains that wholesale production has made this proletariat ready to conceive of wholesale ownership of property, which, carried to its logical conclusion, is social ownership of property.

Thus Socialism, which in Babeuf may be called the most acute manifestation of the democratic revolution ; which in Fourier and St. Simon was the most splendid enlargement of the bold promises of wealth and power poured forth by capital ; which in Proudhon was the sharpest warning given to the societies in process of extinction by the encroachments of bourgeois oligarchy ; Socialism is now in the proletariat, and by its means, the strongest of all the social forces, the one that is continually growing, and that will end by overturning the equilibrium of society for its own advantage ; that is for the advantage of humanity, of which it is now the highest expression.

No, Socialism is not an academic and Utopian conception, it is ripening and developing in closest touch with reality ; it is a great vital force, mingled with all phases of life, and will soon be able to take command of the life of society. To the incomplete application of justice and human rights made by the democratic bourgeois Revolution, it has opposed a full and decisive interpretation of the Rights of Man. To the incomplete, narrow and chaotic organization of wealth attempted by capital, it has opposed a magnificent conception of harmonized wealth, where the effort of each would be supplemented by the co-ordinate effort of all. To the hard pride and selfishness of the middle-class, narrowed by its legalized exploitation and monopoly, it has opposed a revolutionary bitterness, a teasing and vengeful irony, a deadly, implacable analysis that dispels lies and sophistries. And finally, to the social supremacy of capital it has opposed the class-organization of the ever-growing and strengthening proletariat.

How can the régime of class persist when the oppressed and exploited class grows daily in numbers, in cohesion and in self-consciousness, and when it has determined with daily increasing firmness to have done for ever with class-ownership of property.

. . . .

Now at the same time that the real substantial forces behind Socialism are growing, the technical means of realising Socialism are also defining themselves. If we look at the national organization, we see that it is constantly becoming more unified, and more clearly sovereign, and that it has been forced to take on more and more economic functions as a sort of rude prelude to the social property of the future. In the great urban and industrial communes, we see that the questions of hygiene, housing, lighting, education and food are bringing the democracy into ever closer touch with the whole problem of property and the administration of collective possessions. There is also the co-operative movement, including the growing co-operative works for both production and distribution. Also, there are the trade union and professional organisations, that are growing, changing, and becoming more complicated and elastic all the time; trade unions, federations of unions, trades councils, federations of trades, federations of labour.

We have, then, reached a point where it can be safely asserted that the substitute for the privileges of capital is not to be the depressing monotony of a centralized bureaucracy. No, the nation, in which is vested the sovereign social right of property, will have numberless agents, communes, co-operative societies, and trade unions, which will give the freest and supplest movement to social property, in harmony with the mobility and variety of individual forces. There is then a practical preparation for Socialism just as there is an intellectual and social preparation. They are children who, carried away by the work already accomplished, think that all that is now necessary is a decree, a *Fiat lux*, of the proletariat to make the Socialist world rise up forthwith. But on the other hand, those are senseless who do not see the irresistible power of evolution which condemns the unjust ascendancy of the middle-class, and the whole class system, to extinction.

THE RADICALS AND PRIVATE PROPERTY.

DEMOCRACY, under the impetus given it by organised labour, is evolving irresistibly toward Socialism, toward a form of property which will deliver man from his exploitation by man, and bring to an end the régime of class government. The Radicals flatter themselves that they can put a stop to this movement by promising the working-classes some reforms and by proclaiming themselves the guardians of private property. They hope to hold a large part of the proletariat in check by a few reforming laws expressing a sentiment of social solidarity, and by their policy of defending private property to rouse the conservative forces, the petty bourgeoisie, the middle-classes and the small peasant-proprietors to oppose Socialism.

In the first place, to subscribe to such formulas as these means a real intellectual falling off for a part of the democracy. How can men as cultivated as M. Léon Bourgeois and M. Camille Pelletan find any sense in the declaration of the Radical party that affirms " the maintenance of private property? " Used in this general and abstract fashion the phrase " private property " means nothing.

In the course of human evolution private property has many times changed its form and its substance, its meaning and its scope. In the societies that preceded ours, private property embodied itself in forms of oppression which have been definitely abolished. Slavery was one of the forms of private property. In Athens and Rome there were public slaves, slaves of the city or the state ; but most of the slaves were simply a part of the individual patrimony of the citizens. The property in slaves was part of private property. The slaves either cultivated the lands of their Greek or Roman master or laboured for his profit in the city workshops. Individuals owned them, disposed of them, forced them to labor, gave them away as presents, sold them or left them to their heirs. And in the same way, when after the collapse of the ancient society and the Roman régime founded on conquest, slavery was amended to serfdom, the serfs, too, bound to the land, were objects of certain private property rights. Under the Merovingian and Carlovingian kings there were royal slaves attached to the royal lands, and church slaves attached to the church lands, but the immense majority of the serfs belonged to lords who were in the end practically great landed proprietors with a personal property right in their possessions.

During the Middle Ages, from the tenth to the fourteenth century, serfdom was established as one of the forms of what we call private property. It was the lord who disposed of the labour of the serfs. Agricultural serfs, thinly scattered over the great rural domains, and industrial serfs, bakers, smiths, goldsmiths, spinners and weavers, gathered together in the outbuildings of the seignorial mansion, all these were under the domination of an individual ; they were included in his property and sold by him with the estate. They were, like the land itself, like the fields, the vineyards, the cattle, one of the objects upon which the right of private property was exercised.

. . . .

I understand, of course, that slavery and serfdom have been eliminated from private property. But can the Radicals be certain that every element of servitude, oppression and injustice has also disappeared ? And what right have they to use the phrase " private property " in a general and abstract fashion when the elemental meaning of the words varies with the very advance of history ? Formulas like these are the negation of historic evolution. They condemn the party which adopts them to understand nothing and to see nothing. They put it outside the pale of science and of life.

Just as in ancient times private property admitted slavery, and as in the middle-ages it was compatible with serfdom, so to-day it allows the wage system. I am far from wishing to divert myself with the melancholy reactionary paradox of those Socialists who say that the slave and the serf were happier than the wage-earner. The moral and material position of the modern workman is as a whole superior to that of the slave or the serf. We are not talking about that. I simply maintain that to-day private property is embodied in the capitalist form which permits a minority of privileged individuals to dispose of the work, the strength and the health of the working classes, and to levy on them a perpetual tribute. And I maintain that when the Radicals declare in a summary fashion that they wish to uphold private property, either the declaration has no meaning at all, or it means that they want to uphold capitalistic property.

Whoever, in Greece or Rome, had simply announced that he wished to maintain private property, would have announced thereby that he was an upholder of slavery. Whoever, during the Middle-ages, had simply announced that he wished to maintain private or personal property, would have upheld by that serfdom and the system of feudalism. And to-day, when the Radicals, in a general formula, announce to the world that they wish to maintain private property against our attacks upon it, they constitute themselves from that moment the guardians of capitalist property.

But what poverty in these abstract formulas! They do not merely restrain our conception of the evolution of private property when the thing itself is constantly changing ; they simplify it arbitrarily. For from age to age private property not only changes its meaning, but also varies immensely in the matter of greater or less complexity. Sometimes it is applied to social relations that are extremely complex; again, it seems to become more simplified. There are hours when human progress necessitates a complex notion of property ; there are hours when it necessitates a simple one.

. . . .

When slavery was changed to serfdom, property became more complex. The relations between master and slave were of a brutal simplicity. Then, in the Middle-ages, when the serf had a family and a patrimony, the master could not dispose of him so easily. The private property rights of the master in the serf are harder to define, less simple than the rights of the master in the slave. Human personality, which may be said to have been often non-existent in the slave and which was more evident in the serf, complicated the property relation; it introduced varied and uncertain elements into the conception of private property. And in this case, complexity certainly marks a step in advance. On the other hand, at the end of the 18th century, when the hour came for the middle-classes and the peasants to give the death-blow to the feudal system, the Revolution tended to simplify property. It freed industrial property from the binding complications of the guild system. It freed agricultural property from the terrible entanglement of feudal and ecclesiastical dues. The bourgeois and the peasant were more distinctly, more absolutely owners, than they were under the feudal régime; and at that time, during the transition from feudalism to capitalism, the apparent simplification of property was a sign of human progress, just as, twelve centuries before, in the passage from slavery to serfdom, the complication of property had been a sign of human progress.

I read with absorbing interest the excellent work recently published by Giard and Briére, in which M. Henri Sée traces the history of the rural classes and the régime of the great landed estates in France in the Middle-ages. He brings out forcibly the changing complexity and perpetual transformation of property.

"It also appears to be certain," he says in his conclusion, "that in Mediæval times men had a conception of property distinctly different from the one with which we are familiar. We see, at one and the same time, rights over the land exercised by the overlord, the vassal, and the tenant. The peasant, who inherits his right of tenure, may be in a certain sense, considered as a proprietor ; if the rights of the lord were removed, the land he cultivated would belong to him without restriction. The use rights, exercised collectively by the inhabitants of any given estate, might be regarded in some respects as property. That is to say that property in the Middle-ages, has a much more complex character, much less abstract and clearly defined than in our day. *Far from being immovable, the conception of property has been modified in the course of the centuries, and there is no doubt that it will be further modified in the future, that it will follow economic and social phenomena in their evolution."*

There is the broad and far-reaching conclusion to which the French historical school is more and more tending. What force can the scholastic and childish formula of the Radicals have when confronted with the sovereign findings of history and of this living evolution of the conception of property ? Just as it has been modified in the past, the conception of property will be modified again ; and it is certain that it is now going to evolve in the direction of greater complication, of richer complexity. A new force has to be reckoned with, a force which is going to complicate and transform all social relations, the whole property system. This new force is the human individual.

For the first time since the beginning of history, man claims his rights as a man, all his rights. The workman, the proletarian, the man who owns nothing, is affirming his own individuality. He claims everything that belongs properly to a man: the right to life, the right to work, the right to the complex development of his faculties, to the continuous exercise of his free-will and of his reason. Under the double action of democratic life which has wakened or strengthened in him the pride of a man, and of modern industry which has given to united labour a consciousness of its power, the workman is becoming a person, and insists upon being treated as such, everywhere and always. Well, society cannot guarantee him the right to work or the right to life, it cannot promote him from the condition of a passive wage-earner to that of a free co-operator, without itself entering into the domain of property. Social property has to be created to guarantee private property in its real sense, that is, the property that the human individual has and ought to have in his own person.

. . . .

Thus a social property right comes into being for the benefit of the worker, and this right is extended to the many associations—local government units (*communes*), co-operative societies and trade unions—which, from closer proximity to the individual and with greater adaptability than the nation, are able to protect his rights and guarantee his freedom of action, at last secured. In place of the relatively simple and brutal capitalistic form of property, then, will be substituted an infinitely complex form, where the social right of the nation will serve to guarantee, by the intermediary of many local or professional groups, the essential rights of every human being,—the free play of all activities. Every capitalistic element will have disappeared ; no man will be able to make use of other men to create dividends for himself, or profit, or an income, or rent.

But the new property in its vast complexity, national, communal, corporative, co-operative, will be at the same time, individual ; because no individual will be handed over to the exploitation of another individual or the tyranny of groups or the despotism of the nation ; and the rights of each man will be guaranteed by contracts at once adaptable and precise, which, until common property is established will represent private property in its purified form.

So will be verified the conclusion of the historian, that our conception of property is to undergo still further modifications. And in this sense there is not a single searcher after truth, not a single scholar, who is not working to prove the ridiculousness and the puerility of the Radical formula. In M. Sée's volume I read the long list of men of science, historians, workers in the archives and in the ancient charters, who have either gathered together or arranged or interpreted the documents he has used. And undoubtedly, among those men, there must be many who belong, or who think they belong, to the conservative party, some even to the party of reaction. But all, no matter what their personal theories are, no matter what faith they hold, all are serving the cause of evolution, in other words, at the present moment, the cause of Socialism; because they do not stop at the surface of history but penetrate to the depths, and because they reveal to mankind the eternal motion that is continually breaking up and remoulding property according to new forms and new laws. And it is impossible that these studies of the great scholars should not penetrate gradually, through intermediaries, even to the middle-class youth.

So when the Radicals, hoping to put a stop to, or at least impede, the movement of working-class emancipation, speak of the necessary maintenance of what they, in their scholastic jargon, call *private property*, they will find themselves the object on the one hand of the anger of the labour democracy which will justly take them to task for defending the form of capitalists' property under cover of an ambiguous phrase, and on the other of the disdain of science, which will contrast the reality of historic evolution with their abstract and petrified conception of property.

The time is not far off when no one will be able to speak to the public about *the preservation of private property* without covering himself with ridicule and putting himself voluntarily into an inferior rank. That which reigns to-day under the name of private property, is really class-property, and those who wish for the establishment of democracy in the economic as well as the political world, should give their continuous effort to the abolition and not to the maintenance of this class-property.

But let the Radicals note this fact. If their social formula, " maintenance of private property," has become void and meaningless, this result has not been brought about by the example of the past only, or even by the irresistible tendency of new forces to break the capitalistic mould. In bourgeois society itself, in the bourgeois code,* private property appears in such an incomplete form, is so hampered, restricted and broken up, that even now and from the point of view of the bourgeois itself, one must grant that it is either childishness or an anachronism to speak about "the maintenance of private property."

And we Socialists, when we undertake to break up or gradually absorb capitalist property, will often find that we can direct the social movement toward the Collectivist form by simply developing certain practices of bourgeois society, interpreting generously

---

* The code Napoleon.

certain articles of its code, and hastening the forward march of our legislation in the paths along which it has already begun to move. But those who constitute themselves the guardians of *private property* not only deny the society of the future, they misunderstand the society of the present.

SOCIALISM AND THE PRIVILEGED CLASSES.

THE Socialist party ought not, of course, to be a confused echo of discordant interests : it must not allow its thought to be troubled or distorted by the chaos of present conditions. It ought to submit a definite plan to the whole of the people, a definite method of evolution toward a perfectly clear end. But this plan of action must take into full consideration the diversity of elements to be dealt with, their passions, interests and prejudices. These are Liebknecht's exact words :—

> " Necessary as it is to give the freest possible play to all the different groups of interests so that they may be able to express their ideas and their needs, and to allow the people to collaborate in legislation as fully as possible, it would be folly for the Government and for Socialism to abandon all legislation to the initiative of the people.
>
> Socialism should have a definite, easily understood plan, and submit it to the representatives of the people and the different representatives of the interests involved.
>
> Socialist Democracy differs from all other parties in this, that its activity is not limited to certain aspects of the life of the State and social life, but that it embraces all aspects equally, and tries to bring about

order, peace and harmony by reconciling the antagonistic forces in the State and in society.

It is not a party of the great landed proprietors and the feudal interests, and, therefore, it is not, like the Conservative party, constrained to serve the interests of the great and small landowners. It is not a party of the different branches of the bourgeoisie, and consequently it is not, like the National Liberals and the Progressives, bound to serve the particular interests and cater to the love of power of the bourgeoisie.

It is not a party of the sacerdotalists, and it is not therefore bound to further the interests and cater to the love of power of the priest caste, as in the Catholic Centre and the Protestant faction of Social Christianity *à la* Stocker.

It is the party of all the people with the exception of two hundred thousand great proprietors, small proprietors, bourgeois and priests.

It ought then to turn toward the people, and, as soon as the occasion arises, by practical proposals and projects of legislation of general interest, to give positive proof that the good of the people is its only aim, the will of the people its only rule.

It must follow the path of legislation without injuring anyone, but with a firm purpose and an unchangeable ideal.

Even those who now enjoy privileges and monopolies ought to be made to understand that we do not propose to adopt any violent or sudden measures against those whose position is now sanctioned by law, and that we are resolved, in the interests of a peaceful and harmonious evolution, to bring about the transition from legal injustice to legal justice with the greatest possible consideration for the individuals who are now privileged monopolists, and for their situation.

We recognise that it would be unjust to hold those who have built up a privileged situation for themselves on the basis of bad legislation personally responsible for that bad legislation, and to punish them personally.

We especially state that in our opinion it is the duty of the State to give an indemnity to those whose interests will be injured by the necessary abolition of laws contrary to the common good, in so far as this indemnity is possible and consistent with the interests of the whole.

We have a higher conception of the duty of the State toward the individual than our adversaries have, and we shall not lower it, even if we are dealing with our adversaries."

I do not quote these splendid words with the idea of covering my own Socialist policy with the mantle of a revolutionary authority. The Socialist party would be very contemptible and very cowardly if each one of us did not express his own thought without any more support than that furnished by reason alone.

No, we do not need to seek the authority or protection of any one in our effort to find the most convenient road, the broadest, clearest, pleasantest and quickest way of reaching our goal. We make our effort openly, and the proletariat join with us.

And to tell the truth I think that in Liebknecht's own mind these ideas, at once so noble and so practical, were counteracted and clouded by too many different or even contrary theories, to be able to exert a profound and useful influence. I think the time has come to ponder them seriously, and to make them the very foundation of our policy and our theory, instead of only a happy and brilliant accessory. I think that if the Socialist party refused to allow these thoughts to remain general formulas, if it embodied them in a political platform of broad and just evolution toward a well defined Communism, if it gave the impression of being at once generous and practical, ardent in combat and the friend of peace, firm in its opposition to unjust institutions and decided to abolish them methodically, and conciliatory, too, toward individuals, it would hasten the true Social Revolution by 50 years—the Revolution that will be embodied in things, in laws, and in our hearts, not in formulas and words, and it would free the great work of proletarian Revolution from the sickening and cruel odour of blood, of murder and of hate which still clings to the bourgeois Revolution.

. . . . .

But before I leave Liebknecht, I want to quote a few more fragments which show the same high-minded, broadly humanitarian attitude, the same desire for a just and peaceful evolution.

> "In our work of propaganda as in our legislative action, we must never lose sight of the universality of the Socialist conception. . . . .
>
> One side is especially economic, another human and moral, a third political.
>
> We should give equal weight to these three sides in our propaganda and our law-making.
>
> The people should learn by experience that Social-

ism is not only the regulation of the conditions of labour and of production ; that it does not only propose to intervene in the economic functions of the State and of the social organism, but that it aims at the most complete development of the individual and his personality ; that it considers education one of the essential duties of the State, and that its conception of a civil and social ideal is that every individual should embody as fully as possible the ideal human qualities.

The deep significance of Socialism lies in the fact that it unites and fuses the most sublime ideals.

Without the economic side the human ideal would remain in the air.

Without the human side the economic aim would lack moral consecration.

The two are indissolubly united.

They have always been dreamers who have glowed with enthusiasm for the happiness of the human race. But theirs were idle dreams of useless devices, because the material physical means of realising them were lacking. On the contrary the orderly regulation of economic conditions which Socialism wishes to introduce, and which will ensure both an increase in the volume of production and a juster distribution, creates the economic foundation for a human existence in the best sense of the term, the harmonious development of the individual.

Even the advantages of a common ownership of property and co-operative labour were understood in the past, and the very principles of the Community, of Communism, were put into practice, but the human ideal which characterises Socialism was lacking, and historic Communism is rightly judged to have been on a lower grade of civilisation than our present bourgeois society.

Socialism pre-supposes our modern civilisation. It does not go counter to it in any way. Far from being the enemy of civilisation Socialism wishes to extend it to all humanity, whereas now it is the monopoly of a privileged minority.

Since Socialism includes in its domain all the life, all the feelings and thoughts of man it cannot become narrow or exclusive, and this gives it the immense advantage of being able to produce an effect as beneficial as it is harmonious on the whole field of civil and political life.

I add one last quotation showing Liebknecht's care for the details of practical action. Having given several pages to the question of reforms in taxation, he continues :—

"Some people may be surprised that we lay so much stress on the question of taxation.

It is true that if we could pass over to the Socialist State at one bound, we should not need to concern ourselves with taxation at all, because the funds necessary for public expenses would come from the product of social labour. And in a still further stage of development, when all economic functions would be State concerns, there would be no longer any difference between public and private expenses.

But we are not going to attain Socialism at one bound. The transition is going on all the time, and the important thing for us, in this explanation, is not to paint a picture of the future—which in any case would be a useless labour—*but to forecast a practical programme for the intermediate period, to formulate and justify measures that will be applicable at once and that will serve as aids to the new Socialist birth.*

THE PROBLEM OF THE SOCIALIST METHOD.

I DO not need to warn my readers that these articles do not pretend to exhaust the subjects of which they treat. They are obviously only a fragment, or rather the beginning of a larger, more dogmatic and scientific work, in which I hope to define exactly the conception, the policy, and the programme of Socialism at the dawn of the twentieth century.

The studies here gathered together, however, touch with a certain amount of precision and breadth of treatment on problems of the highest importance to our party. This Socialist party is split into factions at the present time, and I might be accused of dreaming of the "mystic units," if I were to say that these divisions were really only superficial. I do not think that they are irreconcilable, but that they come from serious differences of opinion, or rather from serious misconceptions, in regard to the method to be pursued. It is the very development of our party, the growing power of our idea,—I must be forgiven this lapse into optimism,—that have created these differences of opinion by forcing us all to offer some solution of the question of method.

How shall Socialism be realized? That is a problem we cannot evade; and to make vague and uncertain answers is to evade it. Or, on the other hand, if we bring forward in 1901 the answers of our predecessors and our masters of 50 years ago, we deceive ourselves.

There is one undoubted fact which transcends all others. It is that the proletariat is growing, in numbers, in solidarity, and in self-consciousness. The wage-earning and the salaried classes, having increased in numbers and, being organised into groups, have now an ideal. They no longer limit their hopes to the abolition of the worst faults of the present society; they now wish to create a social order founded on a different principle. For private and capitalistic ownership of property, under which one part of mankind dominates the other part, they wish to substitute communion in production, a system of universal social co-operation which shall make of every man a legal partner. Their thought has broken away from bourgeois thought, their action from bourgeois action. They have their own organisation which they put at the service of their Communist ideal. This is a class organisation based on the growing power of the trade-unions and the workmen's co-operative societies, and the increasing share of strictly political power that they have obtained in the State or over the State. All Socialists agree upon this primary conception of the situation. They may assign different reasons for the growth of the proletariat, or at least they may lay different stress on the same reasons. They may magnify either the power of economic organisation or of political activity. But they all realize that by the necessary evolution of capital developed by modern industry, and by the corresponding action of the proletariat, this class has gained an indefinitely increasing power which is called upon to transform the very system of ownership itself. Socialists differ also about the scope and form that the class action of the proletariat should take. Some think that it ought to be involved as little as possible in the conflicts of the social organisation it is to destroy, and that all its energy should be reserved for the final and liberating act. Others hold that it ought to exercise its great human function from now on. At the Socialist Congress held recently at Vienna, Kautsky* brought up the famous saying of Lassalle: "The Proletariat is the rock on which the Church of the future shall be built." And he added: "The Proletariat is not only that. It is also the rock against which from now on, the reactionary forces will bruise themselves." And for my part I say that it is not only a rock, in other words, a compact and motionless

---

* Kautsky is one of the leading Marxists, and is editor of "Die Neue Zeit," the official review of the German party. [Trans.]

force of resistance; it is a vast coherent, but active, force, which mingles in all great movements without being dispersed, and which grows in strength by its contact with the life of the whole. But all of us, no matter what scope or importance we assign to the class-activity of the proletariat, regard it as an autonomous power, which can co-operate with other powers, but is never absorbed by them, and always keeps its own special character for its separate and superior task.

To Marx belongs the merit, perhaps the only one of all attributed to him that has fully withstood the trying tests of criticism and of time, of having drawn together and unified the labour movement and the Socialist idea. In the first third of the nineteenth century labour struggled and fought against the crushing power of capital, but it was not conscious toward what end it was straining; it did not know that the true objective of its effort and the fulfilment of its tendency were the common ownership of property. And on the other hand, Socialism did not know that the labour movement was its living realisation and its concrete and historical force. The glory of Marx is to have been the clearest and the most powerful of those who put an end to what there was of Empiricism in the labour movement and to what there was of Utopianism in Socialist thought. By a sovereign application of the Hegelian method, he united Idea and Fact, thought and history. He enriched the practical movement by the Idea, and to theory he added practice: he brought the Socialist thought into proletarian life, and proletarian life into Socialist thought. From that time on, Socialism and the proletariat became inseparable. Socialism will only realize its ideal through the victory of the proletariat, and the proletariat will only complete its being through the victory of Socialism.

To the ever more pressing question, "How shall Socialism be realized?" we must then give the preliminary answer : " By the growth of the proletariat to which it is inseparably joined." This is the first and essential answer; and whoever does not accept it wholly and in its true sense necessarily places himself outside of Socialist life and thought. And this answer, vague though it is, is not empty of meaning, because it implies the obligation of each one of us to be diligent in helping forward to our utmost the thought, the organization, the activity and the life of the labouring classes. Indeed, in a certain sense, this answer is the only sure one. For it is impossible for us to know with any certainty by exactly what means, in what manner, and at what moment, our political and social evolution will fulfil itself in Communism. But what is certain is that the evolution is hastened, the forward movement vivified, enlarged and deepened by everything that increases the intellectual, economic and political power of the proletariat.

But this first answer, important and valid as it is, is not a sufficient one. Because the proletariat has already grown, and because it has begun to make its power felt in the machinery of economics and politics, the question arises, "What shall be the mechanism by which the victory shall be obtained?" In proportion as the proletarian power realises itself it becomes embodied in definite forms: in universal suffrage, in trade unions, co-operative societies and the various branches of the public service in the democratic state. And we cannot consider the power of the proletariat apart from the forms in which it has already organized itself, the machinery that it has already partially adapted to its own uses. We have, then, reached the time when it is no longer Utopian to try and find out with a certain amount of precision what method Socialism will adopt to realise and fulfil itself. To ask this is not to return to Utopianism or to separate ourselves from the life of the proletariat. It is, on the contrary, to bind ourselves more closely to that life, to grow with it, to shape ourselves by it. For that life is no longer "the spirit moving over the face of the waters"; it is already incorporated in institutions, both economic and political (universal suffrage, democracy, trade unions, co-operative societies) that have reached a definite stage of development and acquired a power and a policy ; and it behoves us to know whether the Communism of the proletariat can be realised and accomplished by these means, or whether, on the other hand, it will only be brought about by a decisive rupture.

To tell the truth, Socialists have always tried to foresee and determine the form and the historical setting of the ultimate triumph of the proletariat. And if we are suffering to-day, if there is uncertainty and uneasiness in our Party, it is because the needs of a new era, imperfectly formulated as yet, are still mingled in one confused mass with the partly outgrown theories of action bequeathed to us by our masters.

Marx and Blanqui both believed that the proletariat would seize power by means of a revolution. But Marx's thought is much the more complex. His revolutionary method was many-sided, and it is therefore his conception that I wish particularly to discuss. In whatever sense one may take it this is superannuated. It proceeds either from worn-out historical hypotheses, or from inexact economic hypotheses.

In the first place Marx's mind was full of memories of the French Revolution, and of the other revolutions in France and Europe that were a prolongation of the first. The trait that all the revolutionary movements, from 1789 to 1796, and from 1830 to 1848 had in common was that they were revolutionary movements of bourgeois origin in which the working-class joined in order to carry them further. In all that long period the working-class was not strong enough to attempt a revolution for its own benefit; neither was it strong enough to take the leadership of the revolution little by little according to the new legal means at its disposal. Two things, however, it could and did do. First, it tried its strength and increased it, by joining in all the revolutionary bourgeois movements; it took advantage of the dangers that the new order had to face, threatened as it was by all the reactionary elements, to become a power necessary to that order. In the second place, when it had grown in power, when hope and ambition were stirring in the hearts of the proletariat, when the different revolutionary fractions of the bourgeoisie were exhausted or discredited by their internal dissensions, the working class tried to take possession of the revolution and turn it to its own uses, by a sort of sudden blow. Thus, in the French Revolution, in 1793, the Parisian proletariat, by means of the Commune, made itself felt in the Convention and sometimes even exercised a sort of dictatorship. Thus, a little later, Babeuf and his friends tried to seize the revolutionary power by a sudden and unexpected move for the benefit of the working class. Thus, again, after 1830, the French proletariat, after having played in the July Revolution the great part noted by Armand Carrel, tried to urge on the victorious bourgeoisie, and by and by to outstrip it.

It was this rhythm of revolution that at first captured the imagination of Marx. Certainly he knew very well, when in November, 1847, he wrote the Communist Manifesto with Engels, that the proletariat had grown; he looked upon it as the true revolutionary power; and it was against the bourgeoisie that the Revolution was to be undertaken.

He writes: " The development of industry of which the bourgeoisie, without either premeditation or resistance, has become the agent, instead of keeping the workers isolated by competition, has brought about their revolutionary solidarity by association. Thus the growth of Modern Industry cuts at the very foundations of that system of production and appropriation of the products on which the bourgeoisie depends. The bourgeoisie is manufacturing as its chief product its own gravediggers. Its ruin and the triumph of the proletariat are equally inevitable."

And again : " The immediate object of the Communists is the same as that of all the other proletarian parties : the organization of the proletariat as a class, the overthrow of bourgeois supremacy and the conquest of political power by the proletariat." And here again is a very definite statement: " We have followed the more or less veiled civil war raging within our present society to the point where that war will break out into open revolution, and where by the violent overthrow of the bourgeoisie, the proletariat will establish its dominion." It is, then, by a violent Revolution against the middle-class that the working-class is to grasp power and realize Communism. But at the same time it seems to Marx that the signal for the struggle is to come from the bourgeoisie itself, which has still to complete its own Revolution. The bourgeoisie will strike at absolutism, or what there is left of it, at feudalism or its remnants ; and when it has given the preliminary impetus by setting free the forces that bring about crises, the proletariat, more powerful to-day than the Levellers of Lilburne were in the English Revolution of 1648, or the proletarians of Chaumette in 1793, will take possession in a revolutionary manner of the bourgeois Revolution. It will begin by fighting side by side with the bourgeoisie, but as soon as the latter becomes victorious, it will expropriate it of the fruits of victory.

"In Germany," Marx and Engels wrote in 1847, " the Communist party will fight along with the bourgeoisie whenever it takes up its revolutionary rôle again ; it will join with it in combating absolute monarchy, feudal ownership of land and the lower middle-class. But it will never forget for a single instant to rouse among the workers the clearest possible consciousness of the antagonism that exists between the bourgeoisie and the proletariat, and makes them enemies. The social and political conditions that will accompany the triumph of the bourgeoisie are so many weapons which the German workman will know how to turn against the bourgeoisie itself. After the downfall of the reactionary classes in Germany, the fight against the bourgeoisie must be begun without delay.

"On Germany especially the eyes of all Communists will be fixed. Germany is on the eve of a bourgeois revolution. This revolution will be carried out under conditions of general European civilization and of proletarian development unknown either in the England of the 17th Century or the France of the 18th. The bourgeois revolution, then, will be necessarily the immediate prelude to a proletarian revolution."

Thus we see that the proletarian revolution is to be grafted on to a victorious bourgeois revolution. Marx's mind, delicately ironical and even sarcastic in tone, amused itself with these tricks of thought. The idea that History was to make sport of the middle-class by snatching the spoils of victory still warm from their hands, gave him a bitter sort of joy. But it was a scheme of proletarian revolution too complicated and contradictory. In the first place, if the proletariat is not strong enough to give the signal for the Revolution itself, if it is obliged to depend on the fortunate chances of the bourgeois Revolution, how are we to be certain that it will have more strength to oppose the victorious bourgeoisie than it had before the movement began? Either the bourgeoisie will be defeated in its attempt at revolt against the old world of feudalism and absolute power, and the proletariat will be overwhelmed long before it has had a chance to fight for its own hand; or else the bourgeoisie will succeed, it will abolish the arbitrary power of kings, of nobles and of priests, do away with feudal property, break the shackles of the guild system, and will then throw itself with so much new life and enthusiasm into the new opportunities it has conquered for itself, that the proletariat will be utterly incapable of creating suddenly another and opposing movement. Even if it acts by violence and surprise, even if it tries to organize a "dictatorship" and to "conquer the democracy" by force, its real power cannot be artificially raised above the level where it was before the bourgeois Revolution.

Miguel was clear-sighted when he wrote to Marx in his famous letter of 1850, foreseeing a continuation of the Revolution: "The labour-party may succeed against the upper-middle-class and what remains of the feudal element, but it will be attacked in the flank by the democrats. We can perhaps give an anti-bourgeois direction to the Revolution for a little while, we can destroy the essential conditions of bourgeois production; but we cannot possibly beat down the small tradespeople and shop-keeping class. My motto is to secure all we can get. We ought to prevent the lower and middle-class from forming any organization for as long a time as possible after the first victory, and especially to oppose ourselves in serried ranks to every constitutional assembly. Partial terrorism, local anarchy, must replace for us what we lack in bulk."

But a lack of bulk is not replaced in this fashion. It is certain that when a class is not yet historically ready, when it cannot act till those whom it aspires to replace have given the signal, and when its Revolution, borrowing power from the movement of its enemy, cannot be called anything but a parasite Revolution, it must continue the revolutionary movements permanently, and keep all the elements of society in continual agitation if it is to attain even a partial success. But this policy only results in giving time and opportunity to the reactionary element that will overwhelm proletariat and bourgeoisie together. These are the tactics to which the working-class is condemned while it is still in the period of insufficient preparation. And if one of the characteristics of Utopian Socialism is that it has not depended on the power of the working-class itself, the Communist

Manifesto of Marx and Engels is still to be counted as a production of that Utopian period. Robert Owen and Fourier counted on the good will of the upper classes; Marx and Engels awaited the fortune of a middle-class Revolution for the proletariat. The propositions laid down in the Manifesto are not those of a class sure of itself, whose hour has struck at last; they are the Revolutionary expedients of an impatient and feeble class, that wishes to force forward by strategy the progress of events.

And even after this paradoxical effort, this proletarian distortion of the bourgeois revolution, Marx does not foresee a complete victory of the proletariat and Communism: he looks for an extraordinary combination of capitalist and communist ownership, of violence to property and organization of credit. Here is a singular fact: after having maintained that it is the evolution of industry and the growth of the industrial proletariat that create a revolutionary force, the Manifesto only foresees as the first move of the victorious Communist Revolution, expropriation of the income from land! In this, Marx is less advanced than Babeuf, whose glory it is to have brought industrial, as well as agricultural production, within the Communist scheme. His position is almost that of St. Just, who seems to have foreseen the possibility of the nation's absorbing the rent of farms. "We have seen above," said Marx, " that the first measure of the working-class will be to constitute the proletariat as the ruling-class, to win the democratic régime."

The proletariat will make use of its political supremacy to wrest by degrees all capital from the bourgeosie, to centralise all the means of production in the hands of the State, (viz : the proletariat organised into a ruling class) and to increase as quickly as possible the total of productive forces of which use can be made.

It goes without saying that this policy implies at the outset despotic inroads on the rights of private property, and on the conditions of bourgeois production. Measures must be taken which without doubt will appear insufficient, and which cannot be regarded as permanent, but which, once the movement is under way, will lead to new measures and be indispensable as a means of revolutionizing the whole system of production. These measures, obviously, will be different in the different countries. Nevertheless the following will be generally applicable, at least in the most advanced countries. (1) Abolition of property in land: application of all rents of land to State expenses. (2) A very progressive income tax. (3) Abolition of all right of inheritance. (4) Confiscation of the goods of all rebels and those who have left the country. (5) Centralization of credit in the hands of the State by means of a National Bank founded on State capital and with an exclusive monopoly. (6) Centralisation of the means of communication and transport in the hands of the State. (7) Increase in the number of factories and means of production owned by the State: the bringing into cultivation of fertile lands generally in accordance with a common plan. (8) Obligatory labor for all; organisation of industrial armies, especially for agricultural purposes. (9) The co-ordination of agricultural and manufacturing industries, preparation of all measures for the progressive disappearance of the distinction between town and country. (10) Free public education of all children. Abolition of the present system of child-labor in factories. Co-ordination of education with material production, etc.

A strange programme, in which are united the agrarian communism of the 18th century and some of the elements of what we call to-day the programme of St. Mandé. In the industrial order, Marx and Engels content themselves at first with the nationalization of the railroads; they do not even suggest the nationalization of the mines, which is accepted to-day by the Radical-socialist party. But what strikes me is not the chaos of the programme, and its mixture of agricultural communism and industrial capitalism. It is not the contradiction between the article that abolishes inheritance, and thus deprives the new generations of industrial capital, and all the articles that allow private property to exist. History shows that different and even contradictory forms have often co-existed; for example, production according to the old guild system and capitalistic production functioned side by side for a long time: all the 17th and all the 18th centuries are made up of a mixture of the two, and free farm labour and serfdom also co-existed for a long time. And I am convinced that in the revolutionary evolution which is to lead us to Communism, we will for a long time be in the juxtaposition of collectivist property and individualist property, of Communism and Capitalism. This is the fundamental law of great transformations. Marx and Engels had a perfect right, without turning round upon themselves, to say in 1872 that they set no great store by their 1847 programme, and this confession was by no means a recantation. " This passage now requires modifications in several directions. The immense industrial progress of the last twenty-five years, the parallel advance of the working class organized as a party, make more than one passage of this programme seem superannuated." At the most, one must be astonished that they did not, in 1847, assign a more important rôle to industrial communism.

But the really amazing thing is that they should have thought the proletariat able to confiscate for its own advantage the bourgeois revolutions, and to "conquer the democracy" by a sudden stroke, and at the same time have supposed it incapable of fully establishing industrial communism, even in the first flush of victory, and in the most advanced countries. The most striking thing in the Manifesto is not the chaos of the programme (which might be unravelled), but the chaos of the method. By a stroke of force the proletariat will have established itself in power at the beginning : by a stroke of force it will have wrenched power from the revolutionary bourgeoisie.

But what does all this amount to? Supposing that the democracy is not ready for the Communist movement, will it not annul, instead of extend the effects of the first dictatorial acts of the proletariat instead of carrying them out and extending their scope? But if, on the contrary, the democracy is prepared, if the proletariat can, by legal measure alone, induce it to develop the first revolutionary institutions in a communistic direction, we have in the legal conquest of the democracy the sovereign method of Revolution. Every other method, I repeat, is nothing but the expedient, possibly necessary for a moment, of a weak and ill-prepared class. And those modern Socialists who are still talking about "the impersonal dictatorship of the proletariat," or who expect a sudden seizure of power and the violation of democratic methods, are reverting to the time when the proletariat was still a feeble element, when it was reduced to adopt artificial means of obtaining a victory.

The tactics of the Manifesto consist in altering for the benefit of the proletariat the course of those movements that it lacked the strength to originate. These are the tactics of a bold force, increasing in strength but still subordinate, and, as a matter of fact, they have been instinctively employed by the working class in all the crises of democratic and bourgeois society. Marx had taken up the idea of the French Revolution and Babeuf. After 1830 the working-class movements of Paris and Lyons prolonged the middle-class Revolution in a confused proletarian affirmation. In 1848 the proletariat of Paris, Vienna and Berlin tried, for a few audacious days, to divert the Revolution in the direction of Socialism. The famous saying of Blanqui: "We do not create a movement, we divert it," is the very expression of this policy. It is the working formula of Marx's Communist Manifesto, the watchword of a class that knows itself to be still in a minority, but called to high destinies. In 1870, the 31st of October succeeding the 4th of September we have another example of the method of Marx and Blanqui.* In the

---

*The Republic of Gambetta was proclaimed on the 4th of September, the day after the news of the Emperor's defeat

Commune itself, the growing activity of the Socialist proletariat substituting itself for the lower-middle-class democracy, is again an application of the tactics of the Manifesto: to graft the proletarian revolution on to the democratic and bourgeois revolution.

. . . .

Thus, in a hundred and twenty years, the method of working-class revolution which Babeuf was the first to apply, which was given a formula by Marx and Blanqui, and which consisted in taking advantage of bourgeois revolutions to introduce proletarian Communism, has been tried or proposed many times and under many forms. It has certainly given great results. By this method the working-class at several great historical crises has become conscious of its power and its destiny. By it, indirectly and obliquely as yet, the proletariat has tested itself in power. By it, the problem of property and Communism has been constantly a question of the day in Europe, according to the advice of the Manifesto: " In all these movements, the question that the Communists bring to the front, as the essential point, is that of property, even if the discussion of this question has not been fully developed at the time."

By following this policy, finally, the pro-

---

at Sedan reached Paris. On the 31st of October an attempt at a proletarian revolution was made, but the insurrectionists had control of the Hotel de Ville for a few hours only.

letariat has taken an active part in affairs long before it had power enough to control them. But it was chimerical to hope that a proletariat Communism could be grafted on to the bourgeois revolution. It was chimerical to think that the revolutionary agitation of the bourgeois would give the proletariat the opportunity for a fortunate stroke. As a matter of fact these tactics have never been successful. Sometimes the revolutionary bourgeoisie has failed, dragging the proletariat down with it. Sometimes the successful revolutionary bourgeoisie has had the strength to restrain and overpower the proletarian movement. And besides, even supposing that a proletarian movement had been suddenly imposed by surprise on agitations of another nature and another origin, what would have been the final result? The strictly proletarian movement would have quickly degenerated by a series of compromises into a purely democratic movement. The very utmost outcome of a victorious Commune would have been a Radical Republic.

To-day, the definite form under which Marx, Engels and Blanqui conceived the proletarian revolution has been eliminated by history. In the first place the proletariat in its increased strength has ceased to count on the favourable chance of a bourgeoise revolution. By its own strength and in the name of its own ideas, it wishes to influence the democracy. It is not lying in wait for a bourgeois revolution in order to throw the bourgeoisie down from its revolution as one might throw a rider down so as to get possession of his horse. It has its own organisation, and its own power. It has a growing economic power, through its trade unions and co-operative societies. It has an indefinitely elastic legal power through universal suffrage and democratic institutions. It is not reduced to being an adventurous and violent parasite on bourgeois revolutions. It is methodically preparing, or better, it is methodically beginning, its own Revolution, by the gradual and legal conquest of the power of production and of the power of the State. And indeed, it would wait in vain for the opportunity of a middle-class revolution in order to strike its *coup de force* and institute a class-dictatorship. The revolutionary period of the bourgeoisie is over. It is possible that, in order to safe-guard its economic interests, and under the pressure of the working-class, the middle-class in Italy, Germany and Belgium, may be induced to extend the constitutional rights of the people, to claim full universal suffrage, real parliamentary government, and the responsibility of ministers to Parliament. It is possible that the combined action of the democratic middle-class and the working-class will everywhere curtail the royal prerogative or the imperial autocracy to the point where monarchy has only a nominal existence. It is certain that the struggle for a complete democracy is not over in Europe, but in this struggle, the bourgeoisie will have an insignificant part to play, such a part for example, as it is now playing in Belgium.

Moreover, in all the constitutions of Central and Western Europe, there are already enough democratic elements for the transition to real democracy to be made without a revolutionary crisis. So that the proletarian revolution cannot, as Marx and Blanqui thought, take shelter behind bourgeois revolutions; it can no longer seize and twist to its advantage the revolutionary agitations of the middle-class, because these are over and done with. On open ground, on the large field of democratic legality and universal suffrage, the Socialist proletariat is now preparing, enlarging and organising its Revolution. To this methodical, direct and legal revolutionary action, Engels, during the last part of his life summoned the European proletariat in famous words which in fact, relegated the Communist Manifesto to the past. Henceforward, middle-class revolutionary action being over, all violent means employed by the proletariat would result only in uniting against it all non-proletarian forces. And that is why I have always interpreted a general strike not as a method of violence, but as one of the most gigantic means of legal pressure that the educated and organised proletariat could bring to bear for great and definite ends.

But if the historical hypothesis from which the revolutionary conception of the Communist Manifesto proceeds, is, as a matter of fact, superannuated ; if the proletariat can no longer count on the revolutionary movements of the bourgeoisie as a means of displaying its own revolutionary power, if it can no longer erect its class dictatorship after a period of chaotic and violent democracy, can it at least expect its sudden installation in power as the result of an economic crash, a cataclysm of the capitalistic system, that has come at last face to face with the impossibility of living, and has suspended payment ? That again was a revolutionary perspective opened by Marx. To establish the class dictatorship of the proletariat, he depended both on the revolutionary political ascendancy of the bourgeoisie and on its economic downfall. Capitalism was one day to succumb of its own accord, under the increasingly intense and frequent action of the crisis for which it was responsible, and by the exhaustion of misery to which it would have reduced the exploited. It cannot be seriously doubted that this was the thought of Marx and Engels in the Communist Manifesto :—

" Hitherto, every form of society has been based, as we have already seen, on the antagonism of oppressed and oppressing classes. But that a class may be oppressed, certain conditions must be assured under which it can at least continue to drag on its life of slavery. Under the feudal yoke, the serf, in spite of his serfdom, did manage to raise himself to membership in the commune (or village organisation), and the member of the lower middle-class managed to develop into a bourgeois. The modern labourer, on the contrary, instead of bettering himself with the progress of industry, sinks deeper and deeper below the conditions of existence of his own class. The workman becomes a pauper, and pauperism increases even more rapidly than population and wealth. It is therefore, perfectly clear that the bourgeoisie is unfit to be any longer the ruling class in society and to impose the conditions of its class circumstances on society as a ruling law. It has become unfit to govern because it can no longer assure to its slaves the subsistence which allows them to continue their slave existence. It cannot help letting them sink to the condition where it has to feed them, instead of being fed by them. Society can no longer live under the rule of this bourgeoisie : that is, the existence of this bourgeoisie is no longer compatible with Social life.

"When matters have got to this pass, when bourgeois and capitalistic exploitation have reached, if one may use the expression, the limit of the human tolerance of the exploited classes, an inevitable revolt, an irresistible rising of the people, breaks out, and the civil war that is latent between the classes is finally put an end to by the "violent overthrow of the bourgeoisie."

This is a true statement of the thought of Marx and Engels at that date. I know that attempts are now made to throw a veil over the brutality of these statements. I am aware that subtle Marxist interpreters say that Marx and Engels only meant to speak about a relative pauperisation. In the same way, when theologians want to harmonize texts in the Bible with proved scientific truth, they say that the word "day" in Genesis means a geological period of several million years. I do not contradict them. Those are exegetical elegances and charities that make it possible to pass without pain from a dogma long professed to a better known truth. And since the "revolutionary" spirits have need of these manipulations, who would dream of thwarting them? Nevertheless, if Marx had only meant to talk of a relative pauperisation, how would he have been able to conclude that capitalism would force its slaves down below the living minimum, and thus, by a series of irresistible reflexes that make it inevitable, the working-class would bring on the destruction of the bourgeoisie?

It has been said, too, that Marx and Engels had only wished to define the abstract tendency of capitalism, to give a picture of what bourgeois society would become by its own law, if the organisation of labour did not, by an inverse effort, counteract the tendency of oppression and depression. And how, indeed, could Marx, who made the proletariat the essence and vital embodiment of Socialism, have failed to recognise and give value to proletarian action? But it seems as if, in the thought of Marx, this action, although in fact ensuring certain partial economic advantages to the proletariat, were chiefly important as a means of increasing its class-consciousness, by developing its sense of injury and of its own strength: " But with the development of industry, the proletariat not only increases in number, it becomes concentrated in greater masses, its strength grows, and it feels that strength more. The different interests and varying conditions of life of the different grades of labour within the ranks of the proletariat itself, are more and more equalised, in proportion as machinery obliterates all distinctions of labour, and reduces wages nearly everywhere to the same low level. The growing competition among the bourgeois and the resulting commercial crises, make the wages of the workers constantly more fluctuating. The unceasing improvement of machinery, ever more rapidly developing, makes their livelihood more and more precarious; the collisions between individual workmen and individual bourgeois take on more and more the character of collisions between two classes. Thereupon the workers begin to form combinations (trade unions) against the bourgeois; they club together in order to keep up the rate of wages; they found permanent associations in order to make provisions before hand for eventual revolts. Here and there the contest breaks out into riots.

"*Now and then the workers are victorious, but only for a time. The real fruit of their battles lies, not only in the immediate result, but in the ever expanding union of the workers.*" This union is helped on by the improved means of communication that are created by modern industry, and that place the workers of different localities in contact with one another. It was just this contact that was needed to centralise the numerous local struggles, all of the same character, into one national struggle between classes. But every class struggle is a political struggle. And that union, for the attainment of which the burghers of the Middle-ages, with their local roads, required centuries, the modern proletarians, thanks to railways, achieve in a few years.

" This organisation of the proletarians into a class, and consequently into a political party, is continually being upset again by the competition between the workers themselves. But it always rises up again, stronger, firmer, and mightier. It compels legislative recognition of particular interests of the workers, by taking advantage of the internal dissensions in the bourgeoisie. Thus the ten hours' bill in England was carried."*

If I have reproduced this pleasant picture of the modern labour movement, it is not with the object of discussing it in detail. It would be necessary to make many reservations on several points, especially that of the levelling of wages. But I wished the reader to put to himself to some purpose the question I ask myself now : " How far did Marx admit that the economic and political organisation of the proletarians would check the tendency to pauperisation which is, according to him, the very law of capitalism." I think the answer may fairly be: "In a very feeble measure." Undoubtedly the workmen grouped as a class and a party are able to gain certain partial advantages, thanks especially to the divisions in the owning class ; but it appears that their union for the fight is the only important gain that they obtain from the fight itself. A general revolt is, then, the ultimate aim that is furthered by the gain in solidarity and the power of protest of the workmen. Their

---

* I have used the English Translation of the Communist Manifesto authorised by Engels and published as a tract by the Social Democratic Federation. In a few minor instances I have altered the phraseology when clearness seemed to demand it. [Trans.]

chances of conducting a revolutionary movement efficiently and of hastening the downfall of the bourgeoisie are thereby increased. But in fact, in the main conditions of their actual life, they suffer under the law of proletarian pauperisation, opposing to it a too feeble counterweight. Undoubtedly this very contradiction between the increasing misery endured by the proletariat, and the increasing power of claiming its rights and of decisive action that organisation was bringing about, seemed to Marx the special motive power of the approaching insurrection, the immediate force of revolution. The concrete ameliorations obtained by working class effort compensate imperfectly for the concrete depreciation of the labourer's standard of life under the law of bourgeois production. In the conflict of tendencies acting upon the proletariat, the depressing tendency has the upper hand at present. It is this more than any other that controls the real situation of the working-class.

And, since we are talking of tendencies, we may note that all the thought of Marx and Engels visibly tended in this direction. I might almost say that Marx needed for his dialectic conception of modern history a proletariat infinitely impoverished and denuded. The proletariat, to fulfil its role of "the human factor" in the Hegelian dialectic of Marx, to represent truly the idea of humanity, ought to be so utterly despoiled of all social rights that humanity, infinite both in distress and right, alone persisted. How can one pretend to understand Marx without penetrating to the dialectic origin, the deep source, of this thought? His " Critique of the Hegelian Philosophy of Rights," which appeared in 1844 in the " Franco-German Annals," is a conclusive document in this connection. "Where," he asks, "does the practical possibility of German emancipation lie? The answer is: it lies in the formation of a class bound by Radical chains; of a class of bourgeois society, that shall not be a class of bourgeois society; of a State that shall be the dissolution of all states; of a sphere that shall have a character of universality, by the universality of its suffering, and that lays claim to no one special right because it is not one special injustice, but injustice as a whole that is being wreaked upon it; that can appeal to no historic title to consideration, but only to the title of humanity; that is not in special opposition to this or that result, but in general opposition to all the principles of the German State; it consists finally in the formation of a sphere that can emancipate itself only by emancipating at the same time all the other spheres of society; that, in a word, is the total degradation of Man and that can, in consequence, realise itself again only by the complete restoration of Man."

I am of course aware that Marx is speaking here of Germany and of the special conditions of her enfranchisement. I know that he recognised in the social classes in France a higher historic idealism ; that according to him they have the habit of regarding themselves as the guardians of the general good, so that for entire emancipation to be effected in France, it would be enough that this idealist action should pass from the bourgeoisie, whose humanitarian mission is limited and counteracted by the cares of property, to the French proletariat, in whom the humanitarian mission can develop to its full and universal significance without any obstacle.

Yes, he is dealing with Germany and the German proletariat. But who does not realise that, in spite of ethnic and historical differences, the German proletariat is, in Marx's mind, the representative, and because of the completeness of its destitution, the typical proletariat?

It is by a Hegelian transposition of Christianity that Marx pictures the modern movement of emancipation. Just as the Christian God humbled himself to the lowest depth of suffering humanity in order to redeem humanity as a whole ; just as the Saviour, to save mankind, had to lower himself to a degree of destitution bordering on animality, a situation beneath which no man could fall ; just as this infinite abasement of God was the condition of the infinite elevation of man, so, in the dialectic of Marx, the proletariat, the modern Saviour, had to be stripped of all guarantees, deprived of every right, degraded to the depth of social and historic annihilation, in order that by raising itself it might raise all humanity. And just as the Man-God, to continue his mission, had to remain poor, suffering and humiliated until the triumphal day of the resurrection, that single victory over death which has freed all humanity from death, so the proletariat is only able to continue its mission in this logical scheme by bearing, until the final day of revolt, the revolutionary resurrection of humanity—a cross whose weight is ever increasing, the essential capitalistic law of oppression and depression. Hence comes the evident difficulty that Marx experiences in accepting the idea of a partial raising of the proletariat. Hence a sort of joy he feels mixed with an element of dialectic mysticism, in summing up the crushing forces that weigh down the proletarians.

Marx was mistaken. It was not from absolute destitution that absolute liberation could come. Poor as the German proletariat was, it was not supremely poor. In the first place, the modern workman embodies henceforward all that part of humanity conquered by the abolition of primitive savagery and barbarism, by the abolition of slavery and serfdom. Then, however feeble at that moment were the claims of the German proletariat to a place of historic importance, they were not entirely lacking. The history of this proletariat since the French Revolution had not been an utter blank. And especially by its sympathy for the emancipatory action of the French proletariat, the workmen of the Parisian sections on the 14th of July, the 5th and 6th of October and the 10th of August,* it shared in the title to historical consideration won by the French proletariat; a title that had become universal in character, just as the Declaration of the Rights of Man had been a universal symbol and as the fall of the Bastille had been a universal deliverance. At the very moment when Marx was writing for the German proletariat these words of mystic abasement and mystic resurrection, the German working classes, and Marx himself among them, were turning their eyes towards France, the great country where the working-class first realized an honourable position. But is there anything strange in the fact that Marx, with his logical and dialectical conception of history, should have given precedence to the tendency toward depression in capitalist

---

* The 14th of July, 1789, is the date of the fall of the Bastille: on the 5th and 6th of October, 1789, the people of Paris, led by the hungry women, forced the King to return from Versailles; on the 10th of August, 1792, the Tuileries were taken. [Trans.]

evolution? Is it astonishing that he should have written again in his "Capital" that "oppression, slavery, exploitation and misery were increasing," and yet also have used the phrase "the resistance of the labouring classes, continually growing in numbers and discipline, united and organised by the very mechanism of capitalist production"—here again balancing a force of depression that acts immediately and a force of resistance and of organisation that seems specially destined to prepare the future?

Engels, for his part, had so strict and rigid a conception of the inflexibility of the capitalist system, of its impotence to adapt itself to the least reform, that he made the gravest and most decided mistakes in his interpretation of social movements. It is difficult to imagine grosser blunders than those that he commits at every step in his celebrated book on *The Condition of the Working Class in England in 1844.* He saw everywhere inconsistencies, impossibilities, insoluble contradictions, which could only be done away with by revolution. In 1845 he announced, as imminent and absolutely inevitable in England, a labour and Communist revolution, which was to be the bloodiest in history. The poor would butcher the rich and burn their castles. No doubt was possible on that score. "It is nowhere easier to prophesy than in England, because here all social developments are extremely well-defined and acute. The revolution *must* come, and it is already too late to propose a pacific solution." Strange conception of that England, always so expert in compromise and evolutionary changes ! He carried his dogmatism in social questions to such a pitch that he ended by adopting toward the specific problems of the time the language of the most obstinate conservatives. All social and political progress under the present system seemed to him impossible just as it did to them. According to him the Chartists had got England into a corner, whence the only issues were either destruction or the complete Communist Revolution. They demanded universal suffrage, but this was irreconcilable with monarchy; they demanded a ten-hours day, but this was irreconcilable with the emergencies of production under the capitalist system, and its effect, excellent indeed, would be to force England to adopt the new methods under the penalty of ruin. " The political economy arguments of the manufacturers," wrote Engels, " that the ten-hours bill will raise the cost of production, that English industry will not be able to struggle against foreign competition, and that wages will necessarily fall, are half true : but they prove only one thing, and that is, that the industrial greatness of England can be maintained only by the barbarous treatment inflicted on the labourers, by the destruction of health, and the social, physical and intellectual degradation of whole generations. Naturally, if the ten-hours bill were to become a legal measure, England would be immediately ruined, but because this law would necessarily lead to other measures that would force her into a course of action diametrically opposed to that which she has pursued hitherto, the law would be a step in advance."

What a spirit of mistrust he shows toward all partial reforms, what narrow limits he assigns to the powers of transformation of the industrial system! And when fifty years afterwards, in 1892, Engels republished this book, he never dreamed for a moment of asking himself by what corruption of thought, by what systematic error, he had been led to such false ideas on the political and social movement in England. He preferred to view with complacency a work to which history had given the lie in almost every particular. It is, then, perfectly natural to suppose that Engels, with this fundamental conception of things, should have always inclined, as Marx did, to give precedence to the forces that in the capitalist system tend to lower the status of the workmen, over those forces that tend to raise it.

But it is not very important what interpretation we give to the obscure and uncertain thought of Marx and Engels on this subject. The essential thing is that no Socialist now-a-days accepts the theory of the absolute pauperisation of the proletariat. All Socialists, indeed, some openly, others with infinite precautions, some with a mischievous Viennese good-nature, declare it to be untrue that, taken as a whole, the economic material condition of the proletariat is getting worse and worse. It must be conceded, after taking account of the tendency to sink and the tendency to rise, that in the immediate reality of life, the tendency to sink is not the stronger. Once this has been granted it is no longer possible to repeat, after Marx and Engels, that the capitalist system will perish because it does not ensure to those whom it exploits more than the minimum necessities of life. It follows from the same admissions that it has also become puerile to expect that an economic cataclysm menacing the proletariat in its very existence will bring about, by the revolt of the instinct of self-preservation, the "violent overthrow of the bourgeoisie."*

---

* It may be convenient for readers if I reproduce here Bebel's remarks on this subject at the Lübeck Congress in 1901. He was answering the attack of Dr. David, whose arguments were practically those of Jaurès.

"The Communist Manifesto has been appealed to. I affirm that already in 1872, Engels, in concert with Karl Marx, declared that they wished to republish it only as a historical document. Whoever has studied the works of Marx and Engels in detail can have no doubt that they never set up the Theory of Increasing Misery in the sense explained by David. If anything is characteristic

Thus, the two hypotheses, one historic and the other economic, from which, according to the ideas of the Communist Manifesto, the sudden proletarian Revolution, the Revolution of working-class dictatorship, would inevitably result, are proved to be equally untenable.

In the political order there will be no bourgeois revolution on which the revolutionary proletariat can mount and ride to victory, nor will there be in the economic order any cataclysm, any catastrophe, which on the ruins of over-thrown capitalism will set up in a single day the class domination of the Communist proletariat, and a new system of production. These hypotheses have not, however, been altogether vain. If the proletariat has been unable to seize the control of a single one of the bourgeois revolutions, it has nevertheless, in a hundred and twenty

---

and refutes large passages in Bernstein's 'Presuppositions of Socialism,' it is the passage from 'Capital,' prefixed as a motto to Bernstein's book, in which Karl Marx describes the Ten Hours Bill as the victory of a principle. Marx took the view that by organization the working class can counteract the depressing tendencies of capital, and if by the strength of their organisation they succeeded in inciting the State to take such steps, then it was not merely a great moral advance, but the victory of a new principle. Even a man like Lassalle, who took so decidedly the standpoint of the Iron Law of Wages,— even he gives no occasion for his being invoked as a witness on behalf of a false conception of the Theory of increasing Misery. In his 'Open Letter in Reply' he says: 'People tell you, workers, you are to-day in quite a

years, forced its way into all the agitations of the revolutionary bourgeoisie; and it will continue to profit under the new forms that democracy is developing by the inevitable internal conflicts of the bourgeoisie. If there has not been a complete and revolutionary reaction of the instinct of self-preservation of the proletariat under the pressure of a complete capitalist catastrophe, there have, nevertheless, been innumerable crises, that, showing as they do the essential disorder of capitalist production, have naturally incited the proletariat to prepare a new order. But the error lies in looking for the sudden downfall of capitalism, and the sudden accession of the proletariat to power as the result either of a great political collapse of bourgeois society, or a great economic collapse of bourgeois production.

It is not by an unexpected counterstroke of

---

different position from that of three or four hundred years ago. No doubt you are better off than the Botokudians or than cannibal savages.' 'Every human satisfaction,' he says further on, 'depends always on the relation of the means of satisfaction to what the custom of the period demands already as bare necessaries for existence, or, which is the same thing, upon the excess of the means of satisfaction over the lowest limit of what the custom of the period demands as bare necessaries for existence.' 'If you compare,' he suggests further, 'what the rich class has to-day with what the working class has to-day, then the gap between the working class and the rich class to-day is greater than ever before.'"— [Trans.]

political agitation that the proletariat will gain supreme power, but by the methodical and legal organisation of its own forces under the law of the democracy and universal suffrage. It is not by the collapse of the capitalistic bourgeoisie, but by the growth of the proletariat, that the Communist order will gradually instal itself in our society. Whoever accepts these truths, which have now become necessary, will soon understand the precise and certain methods of social transformation and progressive organisation. Those who do not completely accept them and those who do not take the decisive result of the proletarian movements of a century really seriously; those who revert to the "Communist Manifesto" so obviously superannuated by the course of events, or who mix remnants of old thought that no longer contain any truth, with the direct and true thoughts suggested by present reality, all such condemn themselves to live in chaos.

SOME SAYINGS OF LIEBKNECHT.

On the 7th of August, 1901, the first anniversary of Liebknecht's death, *Vorwärts* published some very important fragments by him.

Like most journalists who are in the fighting line, Liebknecht was forced to scatter his thoughts, to deal with the daily problems one by one as they presented themselves. But, like many of that profession, too, he cherished the ambition of embodying his essential ideas in a lasting and serious work. His friends found an incomplete manuscript among his papers, in which he had begun, in 1881, to formulate an answer to the great question: *How shall Socialism be realised?* This work gives proof of an indomitable courage in its author, because it was at the very moment when the régime of the state of siege, and Bismarck's still undiminished power were weighing most heavily on the Socialist party, that Liebknecht asked himself, not whether Socialism would triumph, but how it would triumph. And this work shows at the same time his vivid sense of the difficulties to be overcome, the necessary transition and evolution to be gone through.

Here is a fragment of prime importance—
The Realization of Socialism: what measures ought the Socialist party to adopt if, in the near future, it obtains a sufficient influence on legislation.

"I want to answer this question that has been asked," he writes. "But in order that a question may be answered properly, it must first be asked properly. Well, the preceding question has not been well put, at least it is not definite enough. It goes without saying, in fact, that the steps to be taken depend essentially on the circumstances under which the Socialist party has obtained an appreciable influence on legislation. It is possible and even likely, that Prince Bismarck, if he lives a while longer and keeps his power, will come to the same end as his model and master, Louis Napoleon of France. Some catastrophe for which he is responsible may break up the mechanism of the State, and call our party to govern or at least to *share in the government*."

I translate as literally as possible. This means that Liebknecht foresaw, after a great national catastrophe, the total *or partial* assumption of power by the Socialist party.

"This catastrophe may come as the result of an unsuccessful war or an outburst of discontent which the ruling system will no longer be able to suppress. If either one of these alternatives occurs, our party will naturally take other measures and follow other tactics than if it had obtained an appreciable influence without the aid of such a catastrophe.

"We may even imagine, though we can scarcely count on it, that the danger will be understood by those in the upper circles, and that they will attempt to avert a catastrophe, otherwise inevitable, by introducing intelligent reforms. *In this case, our party will be necessarily asked to participate in the government, and will be called upon especially to reform the conditions of labour.* We shall not go further into possibilities; those that we have imagined are enough to show that the kind of action we shall undertake will depend on the circumstances in which we shall have obtained " an appreciable influence."

"But what do we mean by appreciable or sufficient influence? Are we talking about an exclusive influence? of the possibility of our being able to apply our principles, without other limitations than those imposed upon us by economic conditions themselves? In other words, does the question take for granted that we shall have the governing power in our own hands? Or does it simply mean that we shall have an influence over a government formed entirely *or very largely* by the other parties.

"It goes without saying that we should act very differently in the two cases. And within each of the two possibilities we have suggested there are endless degrees and shades of difference, each one of which would call for a different kind of action."

According to Liebknecht, then, writing in 1881, there are two main hypotheses which can be formed when we are considering the possibility of the German Socialist party's attaining power.

Either it would be called upon to act after a great crisis, a national cataclysm, a disastrous war, or outburst of misery, by reason of some profound disturbance, in short, which would sweep away the old forces and would necessarily make way for the new. In this case, it is certain that the action of the Socialist party would be particularly energetic. It would rise up full of power and self-confidence on the ruins of the Imperial order and of the

Imperial parties. And undoubtedly with the aid of this great upheaval, it would be able to accomplish more for the people and the proletariat from the very beginning, than it could do at first if it were called to partial power as a result of the gradual evolution of the institutions of the Empire towards a policy of reform.

But even then, even if a great internal or external storm were to uproot the conservative forces and raise up the power of the people, Liebknecht is not certain that the Socialist party will have complete control. " Events," he says, " will call it to govern or to share in the Government." It may possibly be able to obtain complete control. On the other hand, even after a revolutionary crisis, it may be forced to share the power with other democratic parties. After the German 4th of September, the Socialist party will have a much more considerable share of power in Germany than it had in France after the French 4th of September. But Liebknecht does not feel certain that it will have the whole power—the whole Government. It is possible that it will be forced to reserve a part for the bourgeois democracy. And where will *class-government* be then ?

But there is a second hypothesis : that in which the ruling powers in Germany, feeling the danger, avert the catastrophe by a policy of reform.

> "In this case," says Liebknecht, "our party would be necessarily asked to participate in the government, and especially called upon to reform the conditions of labour."

Liebknecht is not, then, considering a complete assumption of power by the Socialist party on this hypothesis of political and social evolution. Liebknecht could not imagine, and in fact he did not imagine, that under the Empire, under William I., William II., or William III., the Socialist party would obtain from the beginning all the power that perhaps it might be able to grasp, even the day after the fall of the Empire. No, a share only of the power, a share in the Government, will be confided to the Socialist party by those in the "upper circles." But this, Liebknecht considered an imperative necessity. For the policy of reforms to be possible, for it to be efficacious, for it to gain the confidence of the German people, the Socialist party must be called upon to direct it. The party must be represented and given an active part in the government. Liebknecht even goes to the length of almost designating what place in the Ministry it should occupy, and his suggestion bears a strong resemblance to the Ministry of Labour proposed by Citizen Vaillant or the Ministry of Commerce occupied by Citizen Millerand. And Liebknecht says rightly that there will be shades of difference, degrees and numberless forms of this Socialistic participation in the government. As the

Socialist party is more or less powerful and well-organised, as it is able to exercise a more profound influence or inspire more real apprehension, its share of power will be more or less extended, more or less effective; its action on all the non-socialist members of the government with which it will be associated will be more or less decisive, and the reforms themselves will have a more or less marked Socialistic tendency, a more or less distinct proletarian character.

. . . .

The future has never been scanned in a broader spirit; and I consider the publication of these posthumous pages of Liebknecht as an event of capital importance in the political and social life of Germany and the life of universal Socialism.

It is important to understand that Liebknecht foresaw that the Socialist party would obtain partial control of the government even under the Imperial régime. In 1881, during the state of siege instituted by Bismarck, under the coalition of almost all the other parties united in their hatred of Socialism, Liebknecht, whose spirit was bold and serene, foresaw that the Socialists would be called to take office, that the Emperors themselves would be constrained to call them; and he foresaw that the Socialists would not refuse this partial vindication, that they would not refuse to undertake this partial work. Holding themselves ready to profit fully by the Revolution if it should break out as a result of a national cataclysm, they would also, he predicted, be ready to enter into the evolutionary process if destiny decreed that evolution was to be the method of advance. They would be ready, in the interest of the nation, and the interest of the proletariat, to become ministers of the Kaiser.

By what extraordinary phenomenon, by what inexplicable contradiction, did the man who pondered upon and wrote these carefully worked-over pages in 1881, in the full excitement of the revolutionary struggle, by what prodigious upheaval of ideas did this same man condemn so bitterly the entrance of a French Socialist into a bourgeois government ? *

I only hazard the guess that his error in the *Affaire Dreyfus* had upset his judgment on all the events that resulted from it. Almost alone among the German Social Democrats, he was mistaken about the very essence of the affair, he misunderstood its political and social meaning. From the moment he had entered upon a certain line of thought he persevered in it with an inflexibility which was aggravated by his very isolation. The more he found himself alone, the more he persisted that he was right; it was the inevitable other

---

* Millerand was Minister of Commerce in the Waldeck-Rousseau Cabinet. See Introduction.

side to his sovereign qualities of firmness, of energy and confidence. Naturally, then, he suspected or disapproved of everything that was historically associated with an agitation that he had opposed. Since the application of his method of 1881 was made in France under circumstances that irritated him, he did not even recognise his own thought in the progress of events.

Does the fact that he did not publish this work give any one the right to say that it has no value? Involved in the whirlpool of activity, overwhelmed by the business of every day, he had not finished it. But he neither destroyed or disavowed it. Perhaps he had decided that it would be imprudent to surrender his secret thought to the enemy, to tell him the tactics he had planned for the future. Perhaps, too, he was somewhat disconcerted by the events that followed the fall of Bismarck. The great enemy of the chancellor had always magnified, and one might say, satanized, his part. He thought that Bismarck was going to drag the Empire down to the depths, that he would hurl it into some national catastrophe. Well, Bismarck was dismissed in his old age without having compromised the peace of Europe and the solidity of the Empire by a single imprudent act. Liebknecht supposed that Bismarck personified not only the danger but the strength of the Empire. Once Bismarck had fallen he imagined that the Imperial institution would have no further support and would weakly adopt a régime of compromise, under which the Socialist and popular forces would use their strength to such good purpose that they would attain political power. But William the Second, having dismissed Bismarck, was able to preserve the Empire in its autocratic and conservative character, and the Socialist party remained in violent and uncompromising opposition. What point was there then in tracing a programme of action, of Socialist realisation, at a time that was still a period of war to the death, defensive and offensive? That is probably the explanation why Liebknecht had not published this important work, which reveals a whole aspect of his thought. I confess that when I read these strong clear lines I regretted that they had not been known at the time of the International Congress of Paris in 1900. That Congress hailed the great memory of Liebknecht with a sort of piety: perhaps some bitter words would have been softened if it had been known that they struck Liebknecht himself.

LIEBKNECHT ON SOCIALIST TACTICS.

LIEBKNECHT considered that the general tactics of the party were necessarily variable and dependent on circumstances. That method of procedure which of late years has gone by the somewhat insulting name of *Socialist opportunism* has never been more energetically formulated. I translate:—

> " We have now finished with general considerations. Before we begin on details let us briefly resume what has been said.
>
> We have seen that it is impossible to decide beforehand on tactics for our Party which would hold good in every case. Tactics must depend upon circumstances. The interest of the Party is the only law, the only rule.
>
> We have seen that the ends of the Party should be wholly distinct from the means it adopts to gain those ends.
>
> The ends are unalterable; it being of course clearly understood that we may look for a scientific extension, for a correction and a perfectioning of the programme. On the other hand the means of combat and the use that is made of them can change and ought to change.
>
> We have seen that the Party, in order to be capable of the highest possible degree of effective organisation and action, ought to have before all things a clear idea of the essence of our movement, and that it must never neglect the essential for the non-essential.
>
> The essential thing, as we understand it, is that the

unalterable principles of Socialism shall be realised in the State and in society as rapidly as possible.

The non-essential thing is *how* they shall be put into practice. Not that we wish to lessen the importance of tactics. But tactics are only a means of obtaining an end ; and whereas the end presents itself before us firm and immovable, we can argue about tactics. Questions of tactics are practical questions and should be absolutely distinguished from questions of principle.

We have seen in especial that it is absolutely unjustifiable to consider that the tactics of force are the only revolutionary tactics, and to say that he is a poor revolutionist who does not unconditionally approve these tactics. We have shewn that force itself is not revolutionary, but rather belongs to the counter-revolution.

We have seen the necessity of emancipating ourselves from the bondage of certain catch-words, and of developing the power of the Party in the direction of clear thought and brave and methodical action, instead of displaying it in phrases of revolutionary violence, which too often only serve to hide a lack of clearness and vigorous action."

This is great teaching. But if questions of tactics are really of such secondary importance, what is the obstacle to a wide Socialist unity? All Socialists agree as to the aim, the establishment of Socialism, the necessity for a social organisation of property with the object of abolishing all tolls upon labour and of assuring the full development of every human personality.

They disagree as to the means, as to the tactics. Some, who share Liebknecht's opinion, have thought that during the period of the slow dissolution of the capitalist system and of the slow elaboration of the Socialist régime, the Socialists would be necessarily called some day to help to form a government. Others have thought differently. It is a question of tactics, not an essential question. Some, eager to multiply the barriers, have insisted that a constant, systematic and unconditional refusal to vote the budget was an authentic and necessary sign of Socialism. Others have quietly maintained that the party ought not to be bound, and that if a budget included important reforms, and if on that account it was opposed and refused by the reaction, the Socialists, in refusing it also, would be playing the game of the reaction. Here again we have a question of tactics, which will be decided by the very necessities of life and by the political and social evolution—a question hardly serious enough to call forth mutual recriminations and schisms in the party.

And just as tactics are subject to change, the programme, which is after all a part of the tactics, can be modified, revised and completed. For my own part, I think it utterly incomplete and strangely inadequate. I think that it does not correspond any longer to the degree of development of the proletariat, and that it ought to be supplemented by a whole series of measures gradually admitting the working class to economic power, and beginning half-communism in peasant production. Some, on the other hand, object violently to any plan of action which would, as they express it, run the risk of weakening the class instinct of the proletariat by making it a part of the present organisation. We may look for much controversy on this point whenever both sides are willing to think clearly. But here again we are dealing with a question of tactics, that is, as Liebknecht says, a question naturally open to controversy. A schism on this subject is therefore harmful and unnecessary.

. . . . .

If Liebknecht was right, if the appeal to force runs the risk of being counter-revolutionary, if we can and ought to succeed by means of propaganda, organisation, clear thinking and a vigorous manipulation of the law, we ought not to rest content after we have repeated Liebknecht's ideas: we must apply them with method and consistency. Those who talk alternatively of the vote and the rifle, those who, when universal suffrage favours them, give it their allegiance, and when it goes against them, reject it, trouble the forward march of the Party by the incoherence of their thought.

And when I say this I accuse myself as much as anyone else. We all, or almost all, have confused ideas upon tactics, and our action is thereby hampered and weakened.

By our constant use of republican lawful methods and of universal suffrage, we weaken the instinct of revolt and the classical revolutionary tradition of an appeal to force. By our intermittent and purely rhetorical appeals to force, to the rifle, we weaken our hold on universal suffrage. We undoubtedly ought to make a decision, to ask ourselves whether it serves any useful purpose for us to mark the votes cast legally into the ballot box, with a few grains of powder that, however, never explode.

Do we need the majority, and can we win it over to our side? There lies the problem. If the answer is *yes*, then an appeal to force is, as Liebknecht says, *counter-revolutionary*.

Well, Liebknecht answers: *yes*.

I translate again:—

> "We have pointed out, finally, that the Party, in order to put its Socialist ideas into practice, must conquer the power that is indispensable, and that it should do this first of all by means of propaganda.
>
> We have shown that the number of those whose interest forces them into the ranks of our enemies is so small that it is becoming almost negligible, and that the immense majority of those who have a hostile or at least hardly a friendly attitude toward us, only take this position through ignorance of their own situation and our efforts, and that we ought to exert all our strength to enlighten this majority and win it over."

Liebknecht, then, has stated the problem exactly, literally as I state it. What steps ought we to take to win over the national majority to the full Socialist ideal,—through propaganda and lawful action ?

. . . . .

Liebknecht is so anxious to find a broad basis on which he can begin by uniting all the nation, with the idea of then lifting it up step by step to complete Socialism, that he considers even the compulsory insurance laws proposed by Bismarck as a preparation for Socialism. Although in his eyes, the law dealing with accidents is hardly more than a flimsy paper toy, he sees in it a first recognition of Socialist thought.

> "It embodies in a decisive manner the principle of State regulation of production as opposed to the *laissez-faire* system of the Manchester school. The right of the State to regulate production supposes the duty of the State to interest itself in labour, and State control of the labour of society leads directly to State organisation of the labour of society."

That was what Liebknecht said about the law dealing with accidents, which of all the insurance laws is the most superficial, the least intimately connected with the conditions of labour. How much more true is his criticism of the compulsory insurance against old age and sickness, which in fact creates a new right for the working-class, which constitutes a patrimony for the proletariat at once collective and personal : how especially true it would be of insurance against non-employment, which is both necessary and possible, and which would introduce the proletariat into the very heart of the productive system.

. . . .

Liebknecht considers the fact that almost all the parties are obliged to support this proposed legislation, as one of the surest signs of the growth of Socialism in Germany.

> "All the parties," he writes, "with the exception of the most old-fashioned Manchesterian anarchists, who wish nothing less than to resolve the State into atoms and deliver society to the 'free' exploitation of the owning classes, rival each other in their solicitude for the 'poor man' and for the working-class; and there is no doubt that Prince Bismarck, if he wants to, can command a majority in the present Reichstag for his State Socialism. That the Protestant and Catholic clergy, the small farmers and great landed proprietors should accommodate themselves to State Socialism—the priests call it Christian Socialism—is after all not so very astonishing.
>
> But the most striking phenomenon, and one without analogy in modern times, is the attitude of the National Liberals, split into fractions and discredited though they may be, they are an essential part of the German bourgeoisie, they are themselves the typical bourgeois, and to-day have reconciled themselves to State Socialism."

In other words, since the pressure of events and the growing organisation of the Socialist party, the proletariat have finally induced even those classes and those parties which would be naturally most opposed to them to accept the projects of social legislation "which will lead straight to Socialism"; since the immense majority of the nation has allowed itself to be started in the direction of Socialism, and one might say, lifted up to the first step of social organisation, we may conclude that in the same way the immense majority of the nation can be lifted, step by step, by means of an ever more active and definite propaganda, by an ever more energetic proletarian influence, and an ever more effective mechanism of reforms, to the level of our ultimate ideal.

This is Liebknecht's strong and firm conclusion. The great majority of the nation can be won over to our side by propaganda and lawful action, and led to complete Socialism. The whole nation, with the exception of a few refractory but powerless elements, will rise, if we are determined that it shall, by the roads that lead up from bourgeois individualism to State Socialism, and from State Socialism to Communistic, human and proletarian Socialism.

The majority can and ought legally to be ours.

"TO EXPAND NOT TO CONTRACT."

LIEBKNECHT'S thought is full of contradictions. I imagine that his mind, like that of many of the early Socialists, was divided between the uncompromising dogmas of the first days and the new necessities of the larger Party, and that he was not always able to balance these conflicting tendencies.

Liebknecht had begun by being an *antiparliamentary* revolutionist. He had declared and had written that Parliament was a swamp in which Socialist energies would be engulfed. He had said that the platform of Parliament would be useless even for propaganda, because one could preach better in the country itself. But even after the pressure of events and the growth of the Party had forced Liebknecht to discard those formulas, and when he and his friends had entered Parliament, he still kept a memory of his early uncompromising attitude. He reminds us, in the fragments quoted in the *Vorwärts*, that he had objected to a representative of the Socialist Group becoming one of the committee of deans that regulates Parliamentary work. His colleagues did not follow his advice, and they were perfectly right ; because what good would it have done to enter Parliament if, on the pretext of not wishing to compromise themselves, the Socialists had held aloof from the detailed work that alone makes parliamentary action effective !

I only notice this small trait because it symbolises a state of mind. Hampered by the definite words he had spoken in the past, Liebknecht at one time took the attitude of being in Parliament as if he were not there. When, on the other hand, he was considering the conditions under which Socialism could be put into practice, when he tried to read the future in all sincerity and seriousness, he arrived at a very broad-minded conception : he saw Socialism penetrating the democracy little by little, and, by partial and successive conquests, imposing itself even on the Government of middle-class society in the transition stage. Then he was troubled and re-captured by his early habits of uncompromising opposition. And all the doubts and disturbances, the chaos of our modern Socialism, come from the same contradiction between old formulas which are no longer true, but which we do not dare to renounce specifically, and new needs which we are beginning to realise, but which we do not dare confess openly. An example of this sort of contradiction is the fact that Liebknecht, in the very same manuscript in which he foresees the governmental collaboration of Socialism with other democratic factions, nevertheless repeats and seems to agree with the phrase so vigorously condemned by Marx : " From the Socialist point of view, all the other parties form only a single reactionary body." And this is also in direct opposition to the practice of the German Socialists themselves, who do not hesitate to support the Liberal bourgeoisie in their struggle against the small landowners and the remnants of agrarian feudalism. But Liebknecht atoned for the breadth, comprehensiveness, and elasticity of his contribution to the theory of Socialist action, by the dogmatism of this narrow formula.

As a matter of fact, his definition of the working-class is of the broadest :—

"We must not limit our conception of the term 'working-class' too narrowly. As we have explained in speeches, tracts and articles, we include in the working-class all those who live exclusively or *principally* by means of their own labor, and who do not grow rich from the work of others.

" Thus, besides the wage-earners, we should include in the working-class the small farmers and small shop-keepers, who tend more and more to drop to the level of the proletariat—in other words, all those who suffer from our present system of production on a large scale.

"Some maintain, it is true, that the wage-earning proletariat is the only really revolutionary class, that it alone forms the Socialist army, and that we ought to regard with suspicion all adherents belonging to other classes or other conditions of life. Fortunately these senseless ideas have never taken hold of the German Social Democracy.

"The wage earning class is most directly affected by capitalist exploitation ; it stands face to face with those who exploit it, and it has the especial advantage of being concentrated in the factories and yards, so that it is naturally led to think things out more energetically and finds itself automatically organized into 'battalions of workers.' This state of things gives it a revolutionary character which no other part of society has to the same degree. We must recognise this frankly.

"Every wage-earner is either a Socialist already, or on the high road to becoming one. The wage-earners of the national workshops in France, which the middle class government of the February republic wished to make use of against the Socialist proletariat, went over to the enemy at the crucial moment. In the same way we see how those trade unions that were started by the agents of the German middle-class to oppose the Socialist workmen, either have maintained only the shadow of an existence or have in their turn been swept into the current of Socialist ideas. The wage-earner is led towards Socialism by all his surroundings, by all the conditions in which he finds himself. He is forced to think by the very conditions of his life, and as soon as he thinks he becomes a Socialist. But if the wage earner suffers more directly and visibly under the system of capitalist exploitation, the small farmers and shopkeepers are as truly affected by it, although in a less direct and obvious manner.

"The unhappy situation of the small farmers almost all over Germany is as well known as the artisan movement. It is true that both small farmers and small shopkeepers are still in the camp of our adversaries, but only because they do not understand the profound causes that underlie their deplorable condition ; it is of prime importance for our party to enlighten them and bring them over to our side. *This is a vital question for our party, because these two classes form the majority of the nation.* It would be both stupid and ingenuous to exact that we should have a majority sealed and ready in our pockets before we began to apply our principles. But it would be still more ingenuous to imagine that we could put our principles into practice against the will of the immense majority of the nation.

"This is a fatal error for which the French Socialists have paid dear.

"Is it possible to put up a more heroic fight than did the workmen of Paris and Lyons? And has not every struggle ended in a bloody defeat, the most horrible reprisals on the part of the victors and a long period of exhaustion for the proletariat? The French proletariat has not yet fully grasped the importance of organisation and propaganda, and that is why up to the present moment it has been beaten with perfect regularity.

"The lesson of the Commune seems, happily, to have served a useful purpose in educating the proletariat. Our French comrades are hard at work perfecting their organisation and are spreading propaganda, especially in the country districts.

"The German Socialists, on the contrary, have long understood the importance of propaganda and the necessity of winning over the small shopkeeping class and the small farmers.

"*A tiny minority alone demands that the Socialist movement shall be limited to the wage earning class.*

"*The frothy and theatrical phrases of the fanatic supporters of the 'Class-Struggle' dogma, were at bottom a cover for Machiavelian schemes of reactionary feudalism.*

"The hyper-revolutionary parading Socialism, that addresses itself exclusively to 'the horny handed sons of toil,' has two advantages for the reaction. First, it limits the Socialist movement to a class that in

Germany at least, is not large enough to bring about a revolution; and besides this, it is an excellent way of frightening the main body of the people who are half indifferent, especially the peasants and petty bourgeoisie, who have not yet organised any independent political activity."

And Liebknecht put the finishing touch to this thought by the following vigorous words :—

"We ought not to ask, 'Are you a wage-earner?' but 'Are you a Socialist?'

"If it is limited to the wage-earners, Socialism cannot conquer. If it includes all the workers and the moral and intellectual élite of the nation, its victory is certain.

"Why are we forced to stand by now while our friends are persecuted? Why do we have to submit to the most indecent outrages? Because we are still weak. And why are we weak? Because a small part of the people alone understands the Socialist doctrine.

"And shall we, who are feeble, become still more feeble by excluding thousands of men from our movement on the pretext that chance has not made them members of a given social group? Stupidity would in this case become treason to the Party.

"Not to contract, but to expand, ought to be our motto. The circle of Socialism should widen more and more, *until we have converted most of our adversaries to being our friends,* or at least disarmed their opposition.

"And the indifferent mass, that in peaceful days has no weight in the political balance, but becomes the decisive force in times of agitation, ought to be so fully enlightened as to the aims and the essential ideas of our party, that it will cease to fear us and can be no longer used as a weapon against us.

"All legislative measures which we shall support, if

> the opportunity is given us, ought to have for their object to prove *the fitness of Socialism to serve the common good*, and to destroy current prejudice against us."

Thus Liebknecht imagines a whole period of legislative action during which Socialism will have the opportunity of proving its large view of things, when the blindest will be forced to see in it the party of the common good, and during which it will accustom all the finest minds and the noblest consciences, and all the petty bourgeoisie and peasants, to follow it without fear and without shrinking, even to the complete application of its theory and its ideal.

The propaganda of action will in this way supplement the propaganda of speech.

REVOLUTIONARY EVOLUTION.—
AFTER FIFTY YEARS.

When the revolution of 1848 had been crushed everywhere, in France, in Germany, in Italy, in Austria and in Hungary, when the proletariat had been beaten by the bourgeoisie and the liberal bourgeoisie by the reaction, the Communist and working-class party having lost the liberty of the press and the right to hold meetings, in other words, all the legal means of gaining its ends, was forced to enter on subterranean methods and to organize itself in secret societies.

In this way a German Communist society was organized, whose central committee, in 1850, sat at London. Naturally, in these obscure and enthusiastic little societies, embittered as they were by defeat, hot for revenge, and unbalanced by the absence of the steadying contact of ordinary life, puerile plans of conspiracy were abundant. Defeat, however, had not deprived Marx, who was a member of the central committee, of his lucidity, and his large view of life in its complications and its evolution. He opposed childish plans and calmed ebullitions of excitement. But the day came when he had to break away. On the 15th of September, 1850, he resigned from the central committee of London. He insisted upon justifying this act of schism by a written declaration, inserted in the report of the committee, which ran as follows:—

"The minority" (*i.e.*, his opponents) "has substituted the dogmatic spirit for the critical, idealistic interpretations for materialistic. Simple will-power, instead of the true relation of things, has become the motive force of revolution. While we say to the working people—'You will have to go through 15, 20, 50 years of civil wars and wars between nations, not only to change existing conditions, but to change yourselves and make yourselves worthy of political power,' you, on the contrary, say, 'we ought to get power at once, or else go to bed.' While we draw the attention of the German workman to the undeveloped state of the proletariat in Germany, you flatter the national spirit and the guild prejudices of the German artisans in the grossest manner, a method of procedure without doubt the more popular of the two. Just as the democrats made a fetish of the words 'the people,' so you make one of the word 'proletariat.' Like them, you substitute revolutionary phrases for revolutionary evolution."

I repeat it: it is Marx who is speaking. Fifty years! the time that Marx gave the workmen, not indeed to install Communism, but to make themselves fit for political power, have just elapsed. What civil and international wars did Marx have in mind in 1850? What trials did he think the proletariat and Europe itself would have to pass through in order that the working class should reach its political maturity.

Undoubtedly he included the struggle of Western Europe with Russia among the necessary external wars. Russia had just played the part of the great instrument of reaction in Europe, and it seemed to Marx that while Czarism remained unbroken, any revolution in Western Europe would be impossible. So when the Crimean war broke out he hailed it with joy; in his letters on the Eastern Question, he rails at and urges forward the Liberal Ministry in England, who were, according to him, too slow in beginning the fight. Russia was not crushed, and the European Social Revolution did not break out as a result of the Crimean war, as Marx, overtaken himself by that fever of impatience and illusion which in 1850 he had objected to in his colleagues of the London Committee, had for a moment hoped. Nevertheless, the Crimean war did shake the old system in Russia. In that direction, the formidable obstacle that Marx feared is at least diminished, if not destroyed. I think it extremely doubtful whether Russia could now interfere successfully as she did in 1848 and 1849 to crush a revolutionary movement, even if a Socialist revolution were to break out in all Western Europe, if the proletariat were for a moment master of the situation in Paris, Vienna, Rome, Berlin and Brussels, as the democracy were in 1848. I do not know whether the union of the Russian students and the Russian Socialist workmen will be strong enough to force a Liberal Constitution on Czarism for a long time to come. But Czarism, annoyed by all sorts of internal opposition and undoubtedly pre-occupied in strengthening itself within, could not bring to bear on Europe the power that it had at its command a half century ago.

At all events everything that Czarism wished to prevent in 1848 has been accomplished, or very nearly so. Russia had wished to keep Italy divided, subjugated under the yoke of the foreigner; she has freed herself from Austria and from the Pope. And the working-class is becoming one of the principal vital forces in the restored nation. Russia wished to prevent the establishment of democracy in France, even under the Napoleonic form. Well, it is a republican democracy that is firmly planted in France, and that is henceforth invincible. The political and economic action of the organized working-class there grows slowly but surely. In Belgium, the constitution inclines more and more towards democracy, and the proletariat almost grasps universal suffrage. In Germany, by one of those extraordinary ironies of history that bear witness to the invincible power of the democracy, we may say that Russia was unwittingly the instrument that helped forward universal suffrage and Socialism itself. Because Bismarck united Germany for the advantage of monarchist and absolutist Prussia, Czarism twice seconded the designs of Bismarck by a complaisant neutrality, once in 1866 against Austria, once in 1870 against France. Well, in spite of all, Bismarck could only bind Germany together by the tie of universal suffrage; he was forced to make it the golden ring of the new Empire. Moreover, the working-class in Germany, which could not become fully conscious of its unity, and therefore of its existence as a class, in a divided and broken-up Germany, has developed its great political activity over the vast area of a united Germany.

To sum up, the way democracy has grown in Western European States has defeated and still defeats all attempts at violent intervention by the powers of oppression. It is not by any sudden explosion that democracy takes possession of States, and Socialism takes possession of the democracy. The laws by which, from 1860 to 1885 England has obtained an almost universal suffrage are as far-reaching in their effect as revolutions, and yet no one except persons of a certain learning know the exact date at which they were passed. It is like the silent budding of the trees in spring. The new role of the working-class and the peasantry in the national and governmental life of Italy is also the peaceful equivalent of a revolution; it is another *risorgimento*. And the same is true of the many-sided growth of the French proletariat. Czarism can harass and weaken all these movements. It can envelop governments by its diplomacy at once subtle and weighty, but it cannot check the irresistible tendency of nations toward complete democracy, and the irresistible growth of the working class within the democracies.

Thus the obstacle which, according to Marx, had to be done away with before the working-class in Europe could be really capable of assuming political power, has not been destroyed, but has been reduced or evaded. It has been reduced by the Crimean war, which enforced Czarism to be passive during many years, and which made the resurrection of the Italian nation possible four years after, in 1859. It has been evaded by the subtlety of History which disarmed the mistrust of Czarism by introducing German democracy under the auspices of Prussian absolutism. The very ground on which it stands is mined by the growing power of the working-class and Russian Liberalism.

Finally it is evaded and reduced to naught by the continuity of democratic and Socialist growth that is affirming itself everywhere in Europe without the crisis of war.

What other civil or foreign wars did Marx have in mind ? Doubtless he was thinking of the wars that were to free Italy and unify Germany, which the weak Liberal bourgeoisie of the Frankfort parliament had been unable to unite by the bonds of liberty.* Perhaps, too, he had adopted the idea of Engels, who, travelling in France after the days of June, 1848, wrote in his journal that Socialism would only triumph in France by means of a civil war of wage workers against peasants. Happily this is not true. The Commune of 1871 was a heroic struggle of the republican and partly Socialistic workmen of Paris against the country people. But these country people were not the small peasant proprietors : they were the country squires, come out from their small country-houses for the occasion. The democracy of small peasant proprietors did not delay in accepting and acclaiming the Republic. It did not take part in the battle against it. There is no bad feeling between the Socialist workman and the peasant. There will not be any. And we must see to it that no misunderstandings arise in the future, so that the rural democracy

---

* The Frankfort Parliament was held after the Revolution of 1848. [Trans.]

may come over gradually to Socialism as it has come over to the Republic. At all events, the primary condition of working-class political action has been fulfilled in the fifty years that have passed; it has been effected by the trials of great civil or foreign wars, and still more by the slow and continuous pressure of events, by that magnificent *revolutionary evolution* that Marx heralded. This primary condition was the formation, in all Europe, of great autonomous nations, freed from Russian oppression and having attained or tending energetically toward the attainment of democracy and universal suffrage.

Now that that condition has been fulfilled, the working class in Europe, especially the working class in France, is in possession of the " tools and workshop." From that to the completion of the work is a very long way. To-day, as much as fifty years ago, we must guard against the *revolutionary phrase* and set ourselves to understand the deep meaning of *revolutionary evolution* in the new era.

REVOLUTIONARY MAJORITIES.

Those great social changes that are called revolutions cannot, or rather can no longer, be accomplished by a minority. A revolutionary minority, no matter how intelligent and energetic, is not enough, in modern societies at least, to bring about a revolution. The co-operation and adhesion of a majority, and an immense majority, are needed.

It is possible—and history has here a difficult problem to solve—that there have been periods and lands where the human multitude has been so passive and so unstable in character, that it has been moulded by the will of certain strong individuals or small groups. But since the constitution of modern nations, since the Reformation and the Renaissance, there is hardly a single individual who is not a distinct force. There is hardly a single individual who has not got his own personal interests, his ties that bind him to the present, his views of the future, his passions and his ideas. In modern Europe then, for several centuries, every human being has been a centre of energy, of conscience and of action. And since, in periods of transformation, when old social ties are in process of dissolution, all human energies are of equivalent force, the law of the majority is necessarily decisive. A society takes on a new form only when the immense majority of the individuals who compose it demand or accept a great change.

This is self-evident in the case of the Revolution of 1789. It broke out and it succeeded only because an immense majority —one might say the entire country—wanted it. What did the privileged classes, upper classes, and nobles amount to when confronted with the Third Estate of town and country? An atom—two hundred thousand against twenty-four million, one one-hundreth part. And besides, the clergy and nobles were divided and uncertain. There were privileges that the privileged themselves did not defend. They were doubtful about their own rights and their power, and seemed to let themselves go with the stream. Royalty itself, driven into a corner, had to convoke the States General, though it feared them.

As for the Third Estate, the huge mass composed of labourers, peasants, the industrial middle-class, the merchants, the leisured class living on income (*rentiers*), and the artisans, it was practically unanimous. It did not limit itself to protesting against royal absolutism or the parisitic nobility. It knew how to put a stop to all that. The memorials addressed to the Throne all agree in proclaiming that the man and the citizen have rights, and that no prescription can hold good against these immortal titles. And they specify the necessary guarantees. The King will continue to be the chief executive, but the national will is to make the laws. This sovereign will of the nation will be expressed by permanent and periodically elected national assemblies. Taxes shall only be levied when they have been voted by the National Assembly. Taxes will bear equally upon all the citizens. All privileges of caste shall be abolished. No man shall be exempt from taxation. No one shall have exclusive hunting rights. No one shall have the right to appear before a special tribunal. The same law for all, the same taxation for all, the same justice for all. Those feudal rights which are contrary to the dignity of man, those which are the sign of ancient serfdom, are to be abolished without indemnity. Those which encumber rural property and keep it unimproved are to be abolished by purchase. Every employment shall be open to all, and the highest rank in the army shall be attainable by the member of the middle-class and the peasant, as well as by the noble. All forms of economic activity shall also be open to all. The permission of the Guild or the authorisation of the Government shall no longer be necessary before a man can take up this or that trade, create this or that industry, open this or that shop. The Guilds themselves will cease to exist; and consequently the Church maintained as a public service, will no longer have a corporate existence. It will, then, no longer have corporate property. And the estates of the Church, the millions of acres of real estate that it holds, having no longer an owner, since the owning corporation is dissolved, will of right revert to the nation, with the reservation that the latter ensure public worship, education, and public charity.

It is true that the revolution had to have recourse to force—the 14th of July and the 10th of August mark the fall of the Bastille and the taking of the Tuileries. But—and this is a point that should be carefully noted —force was never employed to impose on the nation the will of a minority. On the contrary, force was employed to insure the almost unanimous will of the majority against the factious attacks of the minority. On the 14th of July it was in opposition to the Royal *coup d'Etat*; on the 10th of August it was against the King that the people of Paris marched, and these acts represented the right of the nation, and were the expression of its will. It was not due to stupid submissiveness that all France welcomed the 14th of July with acclamations, that almost all France ratified the 10th of August. It was solely because the force of a part of the nation had put itself at the service of the universal will which had been betrayed by a handful of courtiers, privileged persons and traitors. Thus the use of force was in no way an audacious stroke on the part of a minority, but the vigorous means that the majority took to defend itself.

It is of course true that the Revolution was led on to exceed its first demands, and its opening programme. In 1789 not a single revolutionary foresaw the fall of the Monarchy, or desired it. The very word Republic was almost unknown, and even on the 21st of September, 1792, when the Convention abolished the Monarchy, the idea of a Republic had not altogether ceased to terrify. But the Monarchy did not fall under the assault of a passionate minority, or the formulas of republican philosophy. It was only lost when it became evident to almost the whole nation, after repeated trials, after the royal *coup d' Etat* of the 20th of June, 1789, after the 14th of July, after the King's flight to Varennes, and after the invasion, that the Monarchy was betraying both the Constitution and the Country. Monarchy only fell when the contradiction between royalty and the universal will appeared in all its irreconcilable violence. It is evident then that it was by the necessary and logical action of the universal will, and not by a surprise stroke of the minority, that Monarchy was abolished.

It is undoubtedly true that the revolutionary leaders did not foresee all the economic and social consequences that would result from this act. Mirabeau, for instance, thought that the suppression of royal monopolies and of guild privileges, would bring into being in the new order a legion of small producers, of independent artisans. He does not seem to have understood the great capitalistic evolution of industry. But others saw more clearly, and the Gironde, especially, had forseen that wealth and production (to use an expression of that time) would be like great rivers, the waters of which it would be hopeless to attempt to distribute into little streamlets.

At all events if the Revolution did not know exactly what the secondary and indirect consequences of the economic and social régime that it inaugurated would be, if it did not have a clear understanding either of capitalism, with its combinations, its daring devices, and its industrial crises, or of the antagonistic development of the proletariat, it did at all events know what régime it wanted to inaugurate. That revolutionary France in 1789 was able to have so well-defined a conception of the ends for which it was working and so powerful a will to bring about its desires, was due to the fact that even the boldest reforms that it proposed had either precedents in the past or exact models in real life.

The economic growth of the industrial and

merchant middle-class in the 17th and 18th centuries and the great human philosophic movement of the 18th century had indeed given an audacity and impetus to the public mind which had been unknown before. Nevertheless the memory of the States General of 1614, was a source of light and strength to the men of 1789, in spite of the two centuries of despotism which had intervened. The nation was not going out absolutely to the unknown; it was reviving a national tradition, while enlarging it and adapting it to modern conditions. Moreover, from the point of view of economic life, of agriculture and industry, it did not create unknown types of property and labour. It abolished guilds, and the masterships and wardenships that went with them. But there were already in existence whole regions and particularly progressive industries that were entirely freed from the guild system. In the suburbs of Paris, especially, characterised as they were by special industrial activity, the guild system no longer existed. The beginnings of capitalistic production, with almost unlimited competition, with a variety of combinations, of joint stock companies, sleeping partnerships, etc., had been growing and getting more powerful for several generations. In the agricultural world, too, many peasant holdings had been freed from feudal burdens. The type of independent peasant proprietor, exempt from dues, except possibly the hunting rights of the lord of the manor, had already come into being under the old order. The revolutionary process, then, was really only an expansion, a growth of forms already well-defined and well known.

When it came to the transformation of the Church, the Revolution had strong analogies and vigorous precedents to go upon. The army and justice, which had been feudal institutions in the past, had become in large part State institutions. Why should not the Church as well cease to be a caste corporation and become a State institution? Moreover, even under the old order, church property was considered to be of a special kind, and to be subject to State control. The Revolution cited with great effect the famous royal ordinance of 1749, which forbade the growth of the inalienable property (*mainmorte*) of the Church by legacies. Thus, being subject to the State, Church property was ready for nationalization. Here again, the Revolution had obvious and reliable facts to support it.

In 1789 then, men's minds did not meet in confused aspirations, but in the most precise of positive affirmations. Their wills came together and were harmonised in the full light, the perfect precision of French thought, formed and moulded by the 18th century. And the Revolution of 1789 was the work of an overwhelming and conscious majority.

In the same way and in this case even more

certainly, the Socialist Revolution will not be accomplished by the action, or the sudden stroke of a bold minority, but by the defiant and harmonious will of the immense majority of the citizens. Whoever depends on a fortunate turn of events or the chances and hazards of physical force to bring about the Revolution, and gives up the method of winning over the immense majority of the citizens to our ideas, will give up at the same time any possibility of transforming the social order.

THE NECESSITY FOR A MAJORITY.

I HAVE shown, and indeed the statement is self-evident, that the Revolution of 1789 would have come to nothing except by the will of the immense majority of the nation, and I have said that it is still more necessary for the accomplishment of the Socialist Revolution to have the support of the immense majority of the nation. In bringing out clearly the magnitude of the effort that must be made, I hope not to discourage but to spur on the energy and conscience of those to whom I speak. At all events, if the work to be accomplished is vast, and entails the co-operation of innumerable wills, I shall also show that the resources and forces at our command are likewise vast, and that it only depends on us to march forward to an end both certain and victorious. But I maintain that the vehement effort of a Socialist minority will not suffice, and that we must rally round us almost the whole body of citizens. These are the reasons:—

In the first place, the Socialist minority is not opposed to an inert and passive mass. For a hundred and twenty years, since the Revolution, human energy, already excited by the Reformation and the Renaissance, has been prodigiously animated. In all classes, in all conditions of life, we find active wills, forces in motion. Everywhere the individuals have become self-conscious. Everywhere they redouble their efforts. The working-class has shaken off its drowsiness and passivity. But the lower middle-class is also active. In spite of the often crushing weight of the present economic system, it is not altogether subdued ; it is trying to better itself. And if it often seeks its deliverance by the most reactionary ideas, the most detestable politics, the most sterile and degrading nationalism, it is none the less an active and passionate power. It forms leagues, and in Paris it holds the Republican and Socialist democracy in check. That is to say, it will oppose a resistance that may be effective to any social movement to which it has not been gradually converted at least to a certain degree.

In the same way the small peasant proprietors have played a great role in our history since the Revolution, sometimes on the side of reaction, sometimes on that of liberty. Save for some glorious and fairly numerous exceptions, they took fright at the idea of the Red Terror in 1851, and contributed to the success of the Coup d'Etat and the Empire. Since then they have been gradually won over by the Republic and have become one of the living forces behind it. They are perfectly conscious of their political power. They have begun to hold municipal office, they know that they can make the deputies, the members of the provincial legislatures and the senators, and they would have no tolerance for a great social movement in which they took no part.

I think it extremely short-sighted to say that if the peasants are neutral, that will be enough, that all Socialism asks of them is to stand aside passively. No social force can remain neutral when a great movement is on foot. If they are not with us, they will be against us.

And, anyway, since the collectivist system presupposes the co-operation of the peasants,— for example, they must be willing to sell their produce at the common shop,—their passive resistance would be enough to starve and defeat the Revolution. They know their power and they are not going to let it drop from their hands. Even the economic initiative they have shown for several years, the spirit of progress that animates them, points to the fact that they would not allow their share in great social events to be a purely passive one, when those events will have an immediate re-action on their own lives. Either they will help them, or they will defeat them.

Further, the privileged classes have to-day infinitely more authority, and therefore more power, than the privileged classes before 1789.

The industrial middle-class has remained a vital force. It has followed the laws of scientific progress. It is constantly adopting new methods of production and renewing its machinery. And even from the standpoint of the social struggle, the battle between the classes, it has readjusted its method of warfare; the invention of trade unions of which the employer is also a member and to which he grants special privileges,* is a proof of the audacity and suppleness of its resources. What a contrast between the activity of a great prelate under the *ancien régime*, and a great modern capitalist! Some of these, like certain American millionaires, seem to have inherited the activity of Napoleon. And even in France, in a more modest degree, the capitalist class is ever on the alert. It is not from indifferent and drowsy classes, but from active foreseeing and bold classes, that the proletariat must wring its privileges. How can it do this if it has not the nation on its side? If the mass of the nation is hostile, it will be crushed. And if it is only distrustful, the manœuvres of the capitalist class will soon change that distrust to hostility.

Thus we see that the universal agitation of modern life, the universal activity of energy, no longer admit of successful action by minorites. There are no longer dormant masses

---

* They are called " yellow unions " in distinction to the "red" Socialist unions. [Trans.]

that a vigorous push can shake into life. There are everywhere centres of force which would quickly become centres of resistance, points of reaction, if they were not moving gradually of their own accord in the direction of the new society.

. . . .

In the second place the transformation of property that Socialism wishes and ought to accomplish, is much vaster, more far-reaching and much more subtle than that accomplished one hundred and ten years ago by the revolutionary middle class.

In 1789 the Revolution struck at a form of property marked out by narrow limits. When the possessions of the church were nationalised it was a corporate property very clearly defined that was being absorbed. Outside of the church and of the regular or secular clergy, not a single person who owned property had to fear that the law of expropriation which had been decreed against the church would react on him. The Abbé Maury tried in vain to spread a panic : the bourgeois and peasant proprietors knew too well that the property of the church was clearly defined, and that expropriation would not go beyond those limits.

In the same way, when the Revolution abolished feudal rights, that, too, was a definite measure, with results known beforehand and limited in scope. There were undoubtedly some cases of feudal rights in connection with non-feudal property, but on the whole, the nobles were the only ones affected. The very nature of feudal dues, which presupposed a bond of personal dependence, reserved the benefits accruing therefrom to a single class of persons.

On the contrary, capitalist property is essentially diffused. It has no certain and known limits. It is not concentrated in the hands of a corporation like the Church, or a caste like the nobility. It is, of course, true that the titles that represent it are very far from being as widely dispersed as the made-to-order optimism of bourgeois political economists would have us believe. But it is true that they are not reserved to any given category of titular proprietors and that they are fairly generally distributed. There are small property-owners even in the villages. And if a *coup-de-force* of the minority were suddenly to abolish capitalist property, unexpected centres of resistance would spring into being everywhere. Only by definite and nicely graded steps by which their interests are fully protected, can the medium and small owners be brought to consent to the transformation from capitalist property to social property. And it is perfectly certain that these legal adjustments can only be conducted and these guarantees established by the calm deliberation and legalised will of the majority of the nation.

In the same way the transformation of agrarian property and its evolution toward a system broadly Communistic will be impossible as long as the peasant proprietors are not fully reassured. The adhesion of the peasant proprietors is the more necessary because in comparison with them, the number of large rural proprietors is constantly decreasing. But their adhesion is not to be won by a sudden movement, whose effects they have not been able to calculate. They will only support a movement that has been fully discussed with them, and one that, by constantly raising their productive power and standard of life, will reassure them completely as to the end and object of socialistic action.

And this is not all. In 1789 the Revolution had only a negative work to perform in the domain of property. It abolished, it did not create. It did away with Church property, but the confiscated estates of the Church were put up for sale. It converted them directly into a known form of private property. In the same way, when feudal rights were abolished, what happened was that the property of the peasant was freed of a certain burden, but the fundamental characteristics were not altered. The peasant was simply more fully possessed of that which was already in some degree his. But the Revolution did not bring into being any new form of property. It did not imagine any new social type. Its work of liberty was limited to the breaking of fetters. It did not have to create, it did not have to organise; all society asked of it was destruction; once this destruction had been accomplished, society itself went confidently forward along the route already partly traversed.

The Socialist Revolution, on the contrary must not rest content after it has abolished capitalism; it must create the new type under which production is to be carried on and the relations of property are to be regulated.

Suppose that to-morrow the whole capitalist system is abolished. Imagine that all capitalistic claims on production cease, that the ledger of the public debt is destroyed, that tenants pay no more rent, that tenant-farmers pay no more land-rent, that farmers who hold land as métayers are no longer required to hand over half their produce to the bourgeois proprietor, that all ground rent, all commercial profit, all dividends and industrial profits are abolished; if this destruction of capitalism were not instantly supplemented by a Socialistic organization, if society did not know at once how and by whom labor was to be carried on, what was to be the function of the State, of local government, and of the trade union, and according to what principles the producers were to be remunerated; if, in a word, society was not able to ensure the proper working of a new social system, it would fall into an abyss of disorder and misery, and the Revolution would be lost in one day.

But this new social system cannot be created and inspired by a minority. It can only function with the approval of an immense majority of the citizens. And it is the majority of the citizens that will multiply little by little the germs and tentative undertakings from which the new social order will arise. It is this majority that will gradually create from capitalistic chaos, the various types of social property, co-operative, communal, and corporative, and it will only demolish the last remains of the capitalist edifice when it has firmly established the foundations of the socialistic order and when the new building is ready to give shelter to mankind. In this enormous task of social construction, the immense majority of the citizens must co-operate.

We must never forget the new and grandiose character of the Socialist Revolution. The common good will be its object. For the first time since the beginning of human history, a great upheaval will have for its aim, not the substitution of one class for another, but the destruction of classes, the inauguration of a universal humanity.

In the Socialist order, discipline and the co-ordination of effort will not be maintained by the authority of one class over another, but will come as the result of the free will of associated guardians of the peace.

How, then, can a system based on the free collaboration of all be instituted against the will, or even without the will, of the greater number? All the social forces that were either refractory or inert would be such a drag on Socialist production, would use up so much energy and elasticity in numberless jars and frictions, that the whole system would end in disaster. It can only succeed by the general and almost unanimous desire of the community.

Destined for the benefit of all, it must be prepared and accepted by almost all, practically indeed, by all ; because the hour inevitably arrives when the power behind an immense majority discourages the last efforts to resist its will. The noblest thing about Socialism is precisely that it is not the régime of a minority. It cannot, therefore, and ought not, to be imposed by a minority.

. . . .

I must add that the long exercise of universal suffrage has made it more and more difficult, if not impossible, for the minority alone to carry through any enterprise successfully. Universal suffrage, indeed, is constantly throwing light on the respective strength of the different parties. It is perpetually taking and publishing their measure. For a minority to attempt any movement when all the country knows, and it knows itself, that it is in the minority is, then, extremely difficult.

In 1830 and 1848 the revolutionary minority which rose up could believe, say and make others believe, that it represented the thought of the majority, because this majority, under a system of limited suffrage, was voiceless. I do not speak of the fall of the Empire, whose collapse was due in greater measure to its defeat* than to the Revolution. But undoubtedly the great weakness of the Commune was to have to deal with an Assembly which, reactionary though it was, emanated, or seemed to emanate, from universal suffrage and the general will of the nation.

A minority that, having taken part in the elections and having accepted them as a gauge, should then attempt to do violence to the majority, would be in a false position. And it would be opposed by a majority that, armed with the consciousness of its own force which the authentic figures of the ballot would give, would not yield but in all probability rally to its standard many elements from the revolting minority.

Further, the Socialist Party does not limit itself to demanding universal suffrage everywhere. It wishes universal suffrage with proportional representation. Liebknect, in the fragments published by "*Vorwärts*," demands proportional representation. The Socialists

---
* By Germany. [Trans.]

in Belgium have seconded him. Citizen Vaillant, in a recent article, adheres in principle to the *scrutin de liste*,* under the absolute condition that proportional representation should be instituted. This is also the opinion of Citizen Guesde. But to ask for proportional representation is to ask that each force, each tendency in the country and society should constantly make public its exact numerical strength. It is to wish that the share of electoral and parliamentary influence of each party should be exactly calculated on its actual strength in the country. It is, then, to proclaim all legislation arbitrary that does not emanate from the true majority.

. . . .

According to the confession of every section of the party, then, the Socialist Revolution will be brought about by the will of all of the revolutionary type, by the power of a majority. The partisans of a general strike are the only ones to maintain that the action of the industrial proletariat or even the most active

---

* According to the system of the *scrutin de liste*, the voter, instead of casting his ballot for a single representative of a small electoral district, votes for a list of representatives, which may contain as many names as the whole number to which his County or State is entitled. The system of "proportional representation" is based on the *scrutin de liste* with provisions which ensure that the number of representatives elected by each party is in proportion to its voting strength. [Trans.]

and self-conscious part of that proletariat, unsupported by other sections of the community, would be enough to determine the advent of Communism, the Social Revolution.

THE GENERAL STRIKE AND REVOLUTION.

When we speak of the general strike we must begin by defining the word very clearly. We are not concerned, of course, with the general strike of a single trade. For instance, when the miners of all France decide by the vote of a majority that the time has come for them all to strike to obtain an eight hours' day, a higher pension for old employés and a minimum wage, it is a very important strike, and may be called a general strike of miners. But that is not what is meant by the words "general strike" in the parlance of those who see in it the decisive means of emancipation. They are not thinking of the limited movement of one trade, no matter how vast its extent. On the other hand it would be puerile to say that there could not be a general strike, unless all wage-earners, in all departments of production, quit work simultaneously. The working class is too much dispersed for such unaminity to be possible or even conceivable.

But the words "general strike" have another meaning, very precise, and at the same time very comprehensive. They mean that the most important trades, those that dominate the whole productive system, shall stop work at the same time. If, for instance, the railroad employés, the miners, dockers and long-shoremen, the employés in the weaving and spinning industries, and the building trade employés in the great cities, were to quit work simultaneously, we might say that there was a general strike. Because to bring about a general strike it is not necessary that the whole number of trades should be in line; it is not even necessary that in the trades that are on strike every single workman should go out. It is sufficient if those trades, where the power of capital is most concentrated and the power of labour best organised, and that are therefore the key-stone of the economic system, decide on a suspension of work, and it is enough if they are backed up by such a large number of workmen that the work of those trades is practically stopped.

It cannot be objected that a general strike, if this meaning be given to the phrase, is either chimerical or useless. In proportion to the growth of the labour movement, the possibility of this kind of concerted action is increased. And such action can exercise an enormous influence on the ruling class. It is no longer a single trade, no matter how important, that refuses to work, but a whole union of trades. The movement is no longer, then, a trade movement. It has become a class movement. And could such a movement be barren of important results, organised and carried through as it would be by the essentially productive class, that class for which no substitute can be found, because none exists?

. . . . .

But there must be no misunderstanding on this point. It must not be imagined that there is a magic virtue in the phrase " general strike," and that the strike itself is absolutely and unconditionally efficaceous. A general strike is practical or chimerical, useful or disastrous, according to the conditions under which it takes place, the method it employs and the end it proposes.

There are, according to my opinion, three indispensable conditions for the utility of a general strike. 1st, the working-class must be deeply and truly convinced of the importance of the object for which it is declared. 2nd, a large section of public opinion must be prepared to recognise the legitimacy of that object. 3rd, the general strike must not seem like a disguise for violence, but simply the exercise of the legal right to strike more systematic, vaster, and with a more clearly marked class character.

First, it is essential that the body of organised labour should attach very great importance to the object for which the strike is declared. Neither the decisions of trade union Congresses nor the orders of workmen's committees would be strong enough to drag the workers into a struggle that is always formidable. To brave privation and misery, even with the object of escaping from the situation in which one is sunk, requires great energy. Such energy cannot be roused in an entire class without the influence of really passionate feeling. And passion in its turn is not aroused in men's souls to the degree when it becomes a working and fighting force, except by an interest both very close and very overwhelming, by a very important aim that can be immediately realised.

For instance it is easy to understand how the best organised, the most *self-conscious* trades, educated by a definite and widespread propaganda on the subject, may come to be passionately interested in the eight hours' day, in pensions for old age and accidents, and effective insurance against non-employment. One can imagine that, if the authorities refused to face these questions, or opposed the workmen's solution, enough energy and fervour might be accumulated to bring about the declaration of a great and persevering strike. The working-class is willing to fight for definite and great ends, for positive, extended and immediately practicable reforms. Under conditions such as these, but under no others, the signal given by the labour organisations will be obeyed.

But even if the proletariat is really roused and passionately in earnest, that is not enough. It is not enough for it to follow its own inner impulse if it has not also received a mandate from without. It must have demonstrated to a notable fraction of public opinion that its claims are legitimate and immediately realisable. Every general strike will necessarily bring about disorders in economic relations ; it will upset many traditions and go counter to many interests. The opinion of the mass of the nation (and even of that very considerable portion of the wage-earning class who will not have taken part in the movement) will therefore be very emphatically ranged against those on whom rests the responsibility for a prolongation of the conflict. Well, this opinion will not fix the responsibility on the capitalist class and will not condemn it with any force, unless the justice of the strikers' claims and the possibility of satisfying them immediately, have been clearly demonstrated by an ardent and serious propaganda. It will then express itself against the selfishness of the great owners, the routine of the selfishness of public authorities, and the general strike will result in a notable success. On the contrary if the neutral masses have not been prepared beforehand and partly won over, they will decide against the strikers. And as no force, even a revolutionary one, can hold out against the public opinion of the nation, the working-class will suffer a widespread defeat.

. . . . .

Finally I say that if the general strike is conceived and comes before the public, not in the form of a wider and more perfectly organised exercise of the legal right to strike, but as the forerunner of a movement of revolutionary violence, it will at once set up a reactionary movement of fear which the militant faction of the proletariat will not be able to resist.

This is nevertheless the conception attached to the general strike by the theorisers on the subject. They think that a general strike of the most important trades would be enough to bring on the social revolution, that is, the fall of the whole capitalist system and the establishment of democratic and proletarian Communism. The economic life of the country would be suspended, railroads would be deserted, the coal necessary for industry would remain buried underground; steamers could not even get into the docks where no workmen would unload the merchandise. Everywhere there would be a stoppage in circulation and in production. Naturally great discomfort would result. The workers, in stopping exchange and production, would be starving themselves, and would therefore be forced to adopt violent methods in order to live. They would seize food and other provisions wherever they could lay hands on them. The privileged classes, threatened alike in their persons and possessions, would be shocked and frightened by the inevitable anger of the proletariat whose time-honoured suffering would be intensified by the crisis of misery and hunger. Hence would come inevitable conflicts between the working-class and the panic-stricken guardians of the capitalist system. At the end of a few days, then, the general strike would become purely revolutionary in character. And as the capitalist power would be scattered by the very necessity of keeping watch over the most varied and wide-spread movement, as the army of repression would be scattered and submerged in the flood, the proletariat would be able to overcome the obstacle against which it had hitherto only beat itself in vain, and, master of the social system at last, would install labour as sovereign.

That is the idea. I do not say that it is as clear as that in the minds of all theorisers on the subject of the general strike. I do not say that all who acclaim it attach the whole of this meaning to it. But I do say that for those who see in it the decisive means of liberation, it has that meaning or none.

Well, given this revolutionary meaning, I think the idea is a false one. First, a tactical movement is especially dangerous when it cannot fail *a single time* without involving immense disasters for the whole working class.

The partisans of the general strike, taking the word in this sense, are obliged—understand this clearly—*to succeed the first time.* If a general strike fails after having had recourse to revolutionary violence it will have left the capitalist system intact and armed it with implacable fury. The fear of the ruling classes, and even of a great part of the masses, will express itself in a long succession of reactionary years. And the proletariat will be disarmed, bound and crushed for a long time.

. . . .

But is there, under these conditions, a chance of success? I think not. In the first place the working class would not rouse itself to action in defence of a general formula, such as the advent of Communism would be. The idea of Social Revolution would not be enough to draw them. The Socialistic idea, the Communist idea, is strong enough to guide and co-ordinate successive efforts on the part of the proletariat. It is toward the accomplishment of that end, towards its gradual realization, that the proletariat is directing its organized effort. But if a great movement is to be started, it is essential that the idea of Social Revolution should be embodied in specific claims.

To bring the working class to the point of

leaving the factories and of beginning a battle to the death with all the powers of the present social system, a battle full of uncertainty and peril, it is not enough to cry "Communism" because the proletariat will immediately say, "which Communism, and what form will it assume to-morrow if we win?"

Great movements are never set on foot for the attaiment of remote and vaguely understood ends. They need something solid to work for: they demand a clearly-defined specific issue.

The most practical representatives of the theory of the general strike are perfectly aware of this. They propose to rouse the working class to action in the first place by certain definite and substantial claims. They hope that this movement, when it has become revolutionary in character, as it is certain to do, will expand naturally into complete Communism.

But precisely here lies the essential viciousness of this policy. *It is a trick to entrap the working-classes.* It proposes to drag them by an irresistible mechanical action, far beyond what was indicated to them at first. By the attraction of certain concrete, definite, immediate reforms they are to be led to decide on the great operation of the general strike, and it is supposed that once they have become involved in the network of the machine, they will be conveyed almost automatically to the Communist Revolution.

Now I maintain that in a democracy, this is contrary to the whole spirit of the Revolution. I say that there can only be a Revolution where there is self-consciousness, and that those who construct mechanical contrivances to convey the proletariat to the Revolution, almost without its being aware of what is happening, and fancy that they can lead it to the point desired by a sort of surprise, are going in a direction quite opposite to the real revolutionary movement.

If the working-class is not fully and definitely warned at the outset that it is going on strike for the whole Communist Revolution ; if, when it leaves the mines, the railroads, the factories, the yards, it does not know that it is not to re-enter them until it has accomplished the whole Social Revolution ; if it is not prepared and resolved to the very centre of its being, and from the very beginning, it will be upset during the progress of the movement by the tardy revelation of a programme that was not submitted to its decision before the initial action was taken. And no artifice, no conjuror's trick, will be able to substitute the hidden aim suddenly discovered for the aim that had been avowed at the outset,

To imagining that a social revolution can result from a misunderstanding, and that the proletariat can be led on beyond its depth, is if I may be permitted to use the words, pure childishness. The transformation of all social relations cannot be the result of a manœuvre.

And, if on the other hand, the working-class is prepared beforehand, if it is told in so many words that it is leaving the workshops not to enter them again until it has abolished capitalism, it will be warned by instinct and reflection alike that a society as complicated as ours is not revolutionized by a popular rising of a few days but by an immense continuous effort of organization and transformation. From that moment it will shrink back from an enterprise so vague and chimerical as one would shrink from an abyss.

. . . .

There is still another trick in the tactics proposed by the upholders of a revolutionary general strike. Some of them say : " Perhaps it would not be very easy to draw the proletariat into a deliberately violent movement. It has lost the habit of that sort of thing for many years, and might not throw itself in instantly, at a signal from the militant organizations. The strike, on the other hand, is a perfectly familiar practice of the working-class, and the field of action of strikes is becoming more and more extended. It would therefore be an easy matter to get the working-class to take part in a general strike. In the beginning, this would be only a simple extension of its ordinary habits of warfare.

Besides, and this is an important point, it would be a legal movement. The law permits strikes; it does not and cannot assign any limit to their action. Consequently, the proletariat, in declaring a general strike, would know that it was within its legal rights, and would go into the movement in the strength of that knowledge. Many workmen who would have been shocked at the premeditated use of force and at deliberate revolutionary action, would not hesitate to show their irritation with social injustice by a movement which would be a menace, but would not put them outside the bounds of law in the very beginning and before their blood was up.

"Moreover, what one may call the preventative repressive measures of capitalism, are made impossible by the legal form that the movement would adopt at the beginning. But little by little this general strike, this strike of a class, will necessarily become a great social battle, a revolutionary combat. The spirit of the working people will be roused and their just anger enflamed by suffering, misery, and the inevitable conflicts that will bring capital and labour into opposition all along the line. And even that part of the proletariat which, before the strike was on, would have shrunk from a systematic use of force, will be gradually wrought up to the proper revolutionary heat by the fire of events, by the battle itself and the sufferings it entails. Then we can count on an explosion of the old order."

This, then, if we look at the essential points, is the theory and the hope of a certain number of those who see in the general strike an instrument of revolution. In their minds the general strike is a method of revolutionary training applied to a proletariat too much of whose power would remain inert without the brutal excitement of events.

They do not any longer say to the wage-earner, " Take up your gun." But they think that the general strike, legal at first, will very quickly be led to arming itself with its guns or any other weapon of offence. As a matter of fact, then, they count on the revolutionary force of events to supplement or complete the insufficient revolutionary force of men.

I have a perfect right to say that this is a revolutionary trick. And, like every machine that has not been tested by repeated experiments before it is put to a decisive use, this one leads into error those confiding men who expect everything from it. To work up by artificial means a revolutionary excitement which the ordinary action of suffering, misery and injustice has not been strong enough to produce, is a very hazardous enterprise.

It has been said that revolutions are not decreed. It may be said with still greater truth that they cannot be manufactured ; and that no machinery of conflict, no matter how vast or how ingenious, can replace the revolutionary preparation of events and of minds. It will not do first to postulate the general strike and then expect the revolution to succeed as an inevitable consequence. It is perfectly possible that the proletariat, needing as they do the pretext and even the illusion of legality to lure them into the movement in the beginning, will shrink from the use of force when the pretext is unmasked and the illusion vanished. The die cast into the air may possibly fall on the side of violence; it may also fall on the side of inertia. Now, the dice-box cannot be held in the hand for long, and the game begun again an indefinite number of times. At all events, it is possible that there will be a great deal of haziness, confusion, and contradiction in this movement, the leaders of which will have counted more on the unconscious and obscure force of events than on the resolute force of individual consciousness. At one point, the conflict may, as expected, result in a revolutionary movement; at another, it will keep its legal form and be extinguished in inaction. The revolutionary movement, lacking that principle and solid foundation which the deliberate free-will of men alone can give, will be delivered into the power of local events, and the machinery of revolution will not take hold everywhere in the same way. Hence will come discord, discouragement, and defeat.

It is very true historically that events which were at first limited in scope and harmless in appearance have resulted in vast and unforeseen conclusions. But it is impossible to rely on this growth, and there is no process, not even the general strike, which can inevitably produce the revolution as an outcome of a movement whose beginnings were legal.

Moreover—and this is an especial illusion of many militant socialists—it has not been proved at all that the general strike, even if it does take on a revolutionary character, will force the capitalist system to capitulate. Bourgeois society will set up a resistance proportional to the magnitude of the interests at stake. In other words, to a revolutionary general strike that will require of it the sacrifice of its very existence, it will oppose a resistance up to the limit of its powers.

Now, neither a stoppage of production and transportation, nor intended violence to property and persons, is enough to bring about the overthrow of a society. No matter how powerful one supposes the effects of a general revolutionary strike to be, they can hardly exceed those of great wars and great invasions. Great wars, too, put a stop to, or very much upset, production, suspend or hinder traffic and throw all economic life into a confusion which one might suppose fatal. Yet societies resist these almost deadly crises, these apparently insuperable evils, with the most extraordinary elasticity.

I am not speaking of the Hundred Year's War in France. or the Thirty Year's War in Germany. Then Society kept its form in spite of unheard-of trials—brigandage, sieges, famines, burnings, perpetual fighting and ravaging of whole tracts of country. But in more modern societies, in bourgeois society itself, what prodigious upheavals! Since the last half of 1793 the Society that was the creation of the Revolution has suffered and has even inflicted on itself in its own defence injuries that doubtless no general strike can equal. A considerable proportion of the most useful part of the population, one million five hundred thousand men out of a population of twenty-five millions, are torn from the fields and workshops and thrown to the frontiers. Civil war is raging at the same time as foreign war. La Vendée, Brittany, the South, Lyons, are up and in flames. One half of France is in arms against the other half. A dry and very hot summer has brought a poor harvest. Wheat does not circulate easily, each department, each district wishing to keep for itself as much grain as possible. Although Paris is not invested it is subjected to a real régime of a state of siege: the people have to stand in line at the door of the bakers, regular rations are established; bread is rare. The depreciation of paper money throws all transactions into confusion. But in spite of all these difficulties France keeps enough vital force, revoluntary society has enough spring left, first to defend itself and later to take up offensive tactics again. One can take a city by famine and by force; but a whole society is not captured by these means. It has to deliver itself.

In 1870-71, one third of France is occupied by the enemy; Paris is besieged : civil war follows upon foreign ; a formidable indemnity is imposed on the nation, but notwithstanding all this the deep springs of life are not touched, and the moment peace is declared they gush forth again in marvellous abundance.

. . . . .

And even supposing that a general revolutionary strike does succeed in closing all ports, in immobilizing all locomotives, in destroying railroads, even in occupying as sovereign certain regions that are especially given over to the labouring class and in menacing and reducing the food supply of certain great cities and of the capital ; in spite of all this, ingenious necessity will bring innumerable new resources to light. Consumption and the social life of the community will, if necessary, be enormously reduced, and human nature will accommodate itself to tragic privations, just as at the end of a siege it accommodates itself to a régime the bare idea of which, a few months before, would have made the bravest man tremble. And if bourgeois society and private property will not give way, if the great majority of citizens are opposed to the new social order that the general strike wishes to instal by a *coup de surprise*, then bourgeois society and private property will find a way to live, to defend themselves, and gradually to rally the forces of conservatism and reaction, even in the confusion and disorder of economic life.

Some imagine, it is true, that the general strike, breaking out at many points simultaneously, would oblige the capitalist and proprietary government to spread its armed force over such a large area that it would be practically absorbed by the revolution. This conception is extremely ingenuous. The bourgeois government would devote itself first of all to the protection of the public authorities, the assemblies in which by the will of the majority itself, legal power would reside. If they could not do everything at once, they would abandon to the strikers, if necessary, the railroads and the regions where the Revolution was best organized. They would give their attention to the concentration of their forces and, backed by the enormous power that the will of the legal representatives of the nation would give, they would not hesitate to strike some heavy blow, and would then re-occupy the regions abandoned in the first instance and re-establish communications, just as they are re-established in a few days in a country that an enemy has recently evacuated after tearing up the railroads and destroying the bridges. Even if Paris was for a moment lost to the authorities, as it was in 1871, (and considering the social elements of which Paris is composed, this cannot be taken for granted) it would be enough for them to have a meeting place and to wait in safety, as the King of France waited at Bourges, and M. Thiers at Versailles, the entry of the conservative forces. And they would enter of their own accord without delay. No one should forget that with the shooting clubs and gymnasiums that are so much under reactionary influence, the habits of out-door sports so fashionable in the upper and middle-classes, and the military training of the proprietary classes, these proprietors, the capitalists both great and small, and the angry shopkeepers, would be capable of a very vigorous use of force.

. . . . .

And what would the Revolution be doing all this time? In those regions where it would have seemed victorious at first, it would only be able to eat its heart out on the spot, and exhaust itself in useless violence. The liberal revolutions of 1830 and 1848 had a very definite end in view; to overthrow the existing government and replace it. The revolutionary blows of Blanqui were always calculated to strike at the head and heart. He did not scatter his forces, on the contrary, he concentrated them to attack one or two vital parts of the political system of government.

The revolutionary method of the general strike is the exact opposite. Precisely because it gives an economic turn to the combat in the beginning, it does not supply the working-class forces with a single central aim on which they can unite. They will stay on the spot, at the mouth of the deserted pit, on the threshold of the abandoned factory. Or if the proletarians take possession of the mine and the factory, it will be a perfectly fictitious ownership. They will be embracing a corpse, for the mines and factories will be no better than dead bodies while economic circulation is suspended and production is stopped. So long as a class does not own and govern the whole social machine, it can seize a few factories and yards if it wants to, but it really possesses nothing. To hold in one's hands a few pebbles of a deserted road is not to be master of transportation.

Destruction will be the only resource open to the working class, astonished as it will be at its powerlessness in the midst of an apparent victory. But what good would acts of destruction accomplish except to give a savage character to the rising of the proletariat? Observe that the tactics of a general strike have for their object, and do indeed result in, the decomposition, the infinite sub-division of economic and social life. To stop the locomotives, tie up the steamers and deprive industry of coal, is to substitute the scattered life of innumerable local groups for the unified and general life of the nation. Now this cutting-up and sub-division of life is *exactly counter to the Revolution.*

The bourgeois Revolution was accomplished by federations that drew closer and closer together with Paris as a central bond. Every great revolution presupposes an exaltation of life, and this exaltation is only possible when there is that consciousness of a vast unity produced by the ardent intercommunication of strength and enthusiasm. And the proletariat will accomplish its revolution by the organisation, both in the political and economic world, of strong class representation and class action, which will penetrate and bind together all phases of their life. Division is a return to feudalism. The stoppage of transportation proposed by the supporters of the general strike would force society to revert to the conditions of an inferior civilisation. We should see isolated groups gathered passively about the oligarchical owners and dependent on them for their supply of the accumulated means of subsistence. The rich would be temporary kings, social chiefs and feudal lords in many country districts and small towns. And little by little, all these small sovereignties and tiny oligarchies would co-ordinate their strength to surround and crush the motionless and shame-faced Revolution, that thinking to deprive the Government of all means of communication, would have succeeded only in isolating and breaking up its own forces.

It is, then, perfectly chimerical to hope that the revolutionary tactics of a general strike would enable even a bold, self-conscious and active proletarian minority to quicken the march of events by force. No trick, no machinery of surprise, can free Socialism from the necessity of winning over the majority of the nation by propaganda and legal methods.

Does this mean that the idea of a general strike is useless, that it is a negligible quantity in the vast social movement? Not for a moment. In the first place, I have already shown under what conditions and in what form it could hasten social evolution and the advancement of the cause of labour. In the second place, that such an idea could have appealed to any class as a possible means of liberation ought to be a terrible and decisive warning to society. What! the working class is the main supporter of the whole social order: it is the creator, the producer. If it stops, then everything stops. And one might speak of it in the magnificent phrase that Mirabeau, the first prophet of the general strike, used in the Third Estate, still united then as workmen and bourgeois. "Take care," he cried to the privileged classes, "do not irritate this people, that produces everything, and that, to make itself formidable, has only to become motionless."

The owning and governing class has as yet learned to surrender too small a part of real power to this proletariat, the possessor of such formidable negative force, which at any moment it may be tempted to use. The owners have given, or rather they have allowed the working class to retain, so small a measure of confidence in the efficacy of legal evolution, that this class is fascinated more and more by the idea of refusing to work at all. Labour dreaming of refusing its service, the heart meditating stopping; that is the profound internal crisis to which we have been brought by the selfishness and blindness of the privileged classes, the absence of any definite plan of action on our part. Toward this abyss of a revolutionary general strike the proletariat is feeling itself more and more drawn, at the risk of ruining itself should it fall over, but dragging down with it for years to come either the wealth or the security of the national life.

The general strike, quite powerless as a revolutionary method, is none the less in its very idea a revolutionary index of the highest importance. It is a prodigious warning to the privileged classes, rather than a means of liberation for the exploited classes. It is a dull menace in the very heart of capitalist society that, even if it comes to nothing in the end but an impotent outburst, is witness to an organic disorder that can only be healed by a great transformation.

Finally, if the governing class were mad enough to lay hands on the poor liberties that have been won, the wretchedly insufficient means of action of the proletariat, if they threatened or attacked universal suffrage, if by the persecution of employers and the police they made the right to unite in trade-unions and the right to strike empty forms, then a violent general strike would be certainly the form that a labour revolt would take. It would be their final and desperate resource, more as a means of injuring the enemy than of saving themselves.

But the working class would be the dupe of a fatal illusion and a sort of unhealthy obsession, if it mistook what can be only the tactics of depair for a method of revolution. Apart from those convulsive upheavals that escape all forecast and are sometimes the final supreme resource of history brought to bay, there is only one sovereign method for Socialism : the conquest of a legal majority.

SPEECH AT THE ANGLO-FRENCH PARLIAMENTARY DINNER.

November 26th, 1903.

For me too it is a great pleasure to welcome our guests this evening, and I hail with delight this latest sign, which has been preceded by many others, of the coming together of two great nations.

One hundred and twenty years ago, in the revolutionary crisis that hurried forward the movement of the modern world, they met in a long and violent conflict. But this formidable encounter did not compromise the future. England might have feared the growing and expanding Revolution. She feared that her free commerce and her legitimate influence would be imperilled by a coalition of all the European nations, united by the revolutionary Idea and the revolutionary Sword. And she feared that a violent propaganda would disturb the balance of her own Constitution and would substitute the régime of crises for the strong and continuous evolution that marked her own greatness.

Hence arose a misunderstanding big with storm and peril. Experience, however, has shown that the very Revolution that quickened the free energies of all peoples, increased also the scope and the resources of the eldest of the free peoples. Experience has shown that the ardent force of the French Revolution animated without disturbing the evolution of the English nation : this nation has been able to pass without a shock from the oligarchical suffrage of Pitt to the almost universal suffrage of Gladstone ; it has been able to enlarge the foundations of its public life without disturbing them.

And history itself has done away with the misunderstanding, for though difficulties may arise in the expansion of both nations across the face of the world, the day for irreparable conflicts has long since passed away. Against accidents and surprises we have now to set a friendship that is growing daily in trust and good understanding. It is in the organization of this friendship, if I may use the expression, that we are now engaged.

This friendship is not exclusive, nor is it offensive ; there is nothing secret about it. It not only does not threaten anyone, but it can annoy no one. The trust that exists between us involves no distrust towards others.

Human life, and international life especially, has been saturated with hate, jealousy and deceit for so long, that even to-day, in the midst of profound European peace, there are some minds who cannot see two nations drawing closer together without speculating against whom or against what they are uniting. These people, could not, I suppose, attend a wedding without asking against whom the marriage was directed. No, if the great free peoples, living under the Parliamentary régime, England, Italy and France, join hands and become friends, it is not with the idea of using the advantages of freedom to secure selfish ends. They do it to help on the great European and human alliance, by enlarging and extending national friendships. They do it to serve the cause of civilization, of justice and of peace, in Europe, in the Near East and at last in the entire world.

And the workers of France and England long passionately for this great European peace, the peace of all humanity, stable, well-organized, and permanent. In these quiet and smiling days I cannot forget that a few years ago, at the very height of the crisis that threatened the good relations of the two countries, delegates from the English trade-unions came to Paris and entered into a compact of brotherly friendship with the French unions at the *Bourse de Travail*. And they said then a wise and true thing: that we ought to build up a reserve of confidence and solidarity between the two nations in peaceful years, upon which we could draw during the trials and excitements of difficult times.

This is what we are doing to-day, gentlemen. We are devoting to the cause of peace that faculty of foresight that until to-day, man has reserved exclusively for the service of war. I lately found in our National Library a little anonymous work, published by Johnson, near St. Paul's Church, in 1792, in which the author cries : " The time has come when the silent majesty of misery must be heard." The majesty of suffering labour is no longer dumb : it speaks now with a million tongues, and it asks the nations not to increase the ills which crush down the workers by an added burden of mistrust and hate, by wars and the expectation of wars.

Gentlemen, you may ask how and when and in what form this longing for international concord will express itself to some purpose. I will not hazard a guess this evening. Experience has taught me that one must be prudent when speaking on these questions before one Parliament, and reason suggests that this prudence should be doubled when speaking before two.

Moreover, if we lack modesty and patience we need only remember that in 1790 an Englishman who, before M. Mill, represented the town of Calais, the famous *Conventionnel*, Thomas Payne, wrote in a book that had a great success in France, that England, France and the United States ought to agree to cut down their naval expenses by half, and devote the money thus economised to old age pensions for workmen. But the memory of this plea is already so distant that there is more pathos than danger in evoking it.

And if you press me to risk a prophecy on my own account, I can only answer you by a parable which seems a little strange still and obscure. I gleaned it by fragments from the legends of Merlin the magician, from the Arabian Nights, and from a book that is still unread.

Once upon a time there was an enchanted forest. It had been stripped of all verdure; it was wild and forbidding. The trees, tossed by the bitter winter wind that never ceased, struck one another with a sound as of breaking swords. When, at last, after a long series of freezing nights and sunless days that seemed like nights, all living things trembled with the first call of spring, the trees became afraid of the sap that began to move within them. And the solitary and bitter spirit that had its dwelling within the hard bark of each of them, said very low, with a shudder that came up from the deepest roots :—

"Have a care; if thou art the first to risk yielding to the wooing of the new season, if thou art the first to turn thy lance-like buds into blossoms and leaves, their delicate raiment will be torn by the rough blows of the trees that have been slower to put forth leaves and flowers."

And the proud and melancholy spirit that was shut up within the great Druidical oak spoke to its tree with peculiar insistence: "Wilt thou, too, seek to join the universal love-feast, thou whose noble branches have been broken by the storm?"

Thus, in the enchanted forest, mutual distrust drove back the sap, and prolonged the death-like winter even after the call of spring.

What happened at last? By what mysterious influence was the grim charm broken? Did some tree find the courage to act alone, like those April poplars that break into a shower of verdure and give from afar the signal for a renewal of all life? Or did a warmer and more life-giving beam start the sap moving in all the trees at once? For lo! in a single day the whole forest burst forth into a magnificent flowering of joy and peace.

Gentlemen, if you will allow me to fit my toast to this old allegory, and to give it before you and with you the form of an invocation to Nature, I will drink to the sunbeam that charmed the whole forest into bloom.

MOONLIGHT.

I was walking the other evening in the country, and talking with a young friend who had just graduated among the first of his class at the *Ecole Polytechnique*, after having done very good work in literature, and who is as broad minded as he is keen.

Our way led over a broad upland, shut in on the left by low rounded hills which were separated by ravine-like meadows. The full moon lit up the fresh, clear space, and the pale distant stars shone with a tender sweetness. The road, white under the radiance, stretched out straight before us and was lost far away in the mystery of the horizon, bathed in light and shadow. It seemed to lead from reality to dreamland.

"Yes," I said to him, "the thing that angers me in our present Society is not only the physical suffering that might be mitigated by another régime, but the moral suffering that is brought by a state of warfare and monstrous inequality.

"To labour should be a natural function and a joy: often it is nothing more than servitude and suffering. It ought to be the war waged by all mankind united against inanimate things, against the fatalities of nature and the difficulties of life; it is the war of man with man Men spend their days struggling to take from one another the joys of life by fraud, by the arts of bitter greed, the oppression of the weak, and all the violent methods of unlimited competition. Even among those who are called happy there are few who are really happy, because the brutal conditions of life hold them in their grip: they hardly have the right to be just and kind under pain of ruin. In the universal warfare, some are the slaves of their fortune as others are the slaves of their poverty. Yes, above and below, our present social order produces nothing but slaves, because those men are not free who have neither the time nor the strength to follow the noblest instincts of their minds and their souls.

"And if you look at the lower grades, what poverty you see, I don't say in the means of life, but in life itself! Look at the millions of labourers; they work in the factories and in the workshops, yet they have no right whatever in those factories and workshops: they can be turned out to-morrow. Neither have they any right over the machine they tend, no share of ownership in the immense tool that humanity has bit by bit created for itself. They are strangers in the organised power of the world: they are almost strangers in the civilisation of the world.

"In the mines, the canals, the railroads, the ports, the prodigious applications of steam and electricity, and all the great enterprises that develop the power and the pride of man, they have no part, no part at all, except that of inert instruments. They have no seat in the councils that decide on new undertakings and direct them; these are entirely in the hands of a limited class which knows all the joys of intellectual activity and hardy initiative, just as it possesses all the pleasures of wealth, and which would be happy if it were permitted to man to be happy apart from human solidarity. There are millions of labourers who are reduced to an inert and mechanical existence. And, terrifying as the idea is, if to-morrow machines could be substituted for them, nothing would be changed in human existence.

"When, on the contrary, Socialism has triumphed, when conditions of peace have succeeded to conditions of combat, when all men have their share of property in the immense human capital and their share of initiative and of the exercise of free-will in the immense human activity, then all men will know the fulness of pride and joy; and they will feel that they are co-operators in the universal civilisation, even if their immediate contribution is only the humblest manual labour; and this labour, more noble and more fraternal in character, will be so regulated that the labourers shall always reserve for themselves some leisure hours for reflection and for a cultivation of the sense of life.

" They will have a better understanding of the hidden meaning of life, whose mysterious aim is the harmony of all consciences, of all forces, and of all liberties. They will understand history better and will love it, because it will be their history, since they are the heirs of the whole human race. Finally, they will understand the universe better, because when they see conscience and spirit triumphing in humanity, they will be quick to feel that this universe which has given birth to humanity cannot be fundamentally brutal and blind, that there is spirit everywhere, soul everywhere, and that the universe itself is simply an immense confused aspiration toward order, beauty, freedom, and goodness. Their point of view will be changed : they will look with new eyes not only at their brother men, but at the earth and the sky, rocks and trees, animals, flowers and stars.

" And that is why we have a right to think of these things in the open fields and under the starlit sky. Yes, we can call the sublime night to witness to our sublime hopes, the night in which new worlds are being formed in secret, and we can mingle the immense gentleness and sweetness of peaceful nature with our vision of human gentleness and sweetness."

"Well and good," answered my young engineer, "but why don't you simply talk about social progress ; why do you bring in Socialism ? Social progress is a real thing, whereas Socialism is nothing but a word. It is the name of a small, but very vehement or rather violent sect, which is, moreover, divided against itself : it is not a serious force making for progress. Possibly the solutions which the Socialists propose will be gradually adopted, but their triumph will not be due to the Socialists. There will never be a Government acting and legislating in the name of Socialism, because a Government has to base its action on existing facts, even when it is reforming the present order or creating a new order. Well, Socialism poses as an overwhelming revelation, a new gospel, that looks to the future itself for the basis on which to build the future.

"As a matter of fact, all the elements of the problem exist already in our present society, and the solution is indicated or even roughly sketched in : the solution of the social problem is wholly comprised in political liberty, the development of popular education, and the right of labour to organise. Well, political liberty exists, education, and an education always more advanced, is becoming more and more diffused in the labour world, and the workers have the right to organise.

" When they are better educated they will

begin by taking part through their imagination and their intelligence in all great human undertakings; and when their personal subjective value has been increased in this way, it will react of its own accord on the social régime by an irresistible action from within outward. For instance, if all the children of the lower classes acquire the taste and the need for reading, if their education has been vital and effective enough to bring about this result, it is impossible that this universal need shall not in the end, by a more economical regulation of the work, insure to the workers some hours of leisure for the pleasures of the mind. Moreover, when they understand the mechanism of production and exchange better, when they know exactly what conditions obtain in manufacture generally, and in their industry in particular, what its markets are, what capital is invested in it, and how much more capital could be profitably employed in its development, then these men, free, organised, and well educated as they will be, will by the very nature of things begin to be admitted as members of the boards of directors of the great corporations, and afterwards little by little to the management of ordinary business concerns. The next step will be profit-sharing and a share of authority and of economic power.

" But I repeat, all this will be accomplished without the aid of any high-sounding formulas, and we shall find that we have arrived at the end of Socialism without ever having come across Socialism on the way. Old sailors make the new hands believe that when they go from one pole to the other they have to pass over the line of the equator, stretched taut and firm on the surface of the sea. No, the line is never seen, and unless most minute calculations are made we cross it without having any idea that we have done so: in the same way we shall cross the Socialist equator.

" The revolutionaries of 1848 for whom you appear to cherish an affection, were generous but extremely annoying. They never spoke of the Future without a capital letter, and they contrasted the Past and the Present as though they were respectively an archangel of light and a demon from the pit. They were constantly feeling the breath of the future pass in their long hair, and thrill through their long beards. They looked for the man of the future, the society of the future, the science of the future, the art of the future, the religion of the future. I even believe they thought the modest sun that gives us light a very mediocre very bourgeois, sort of star, and that they were looking for the sun of the future.

"It always seemed to them that souls inflamed and burning with zeal were going to raise up a new social order, as the internal fire in our earth can raise up new mountain peaks;

and there was not a little pride mingled with this hope, because they had made up their minds beforehand that they were to be the managers or directors of the new society, and the new mountain tops were to be their pedestal. What illusions of generosity! what chimeras of vanity! The main form of human society, like that of earth itself, is fairly definitely established; there will be transformations, but not any vast metamorphoses. There will not be a social upheaval any more than there will be a geological upheaval.

"Human progress has entered upon its silent period, which is not the least productive. Pascal used to say, when he looked at the sky spread out above our heads: "The eternal silence of those infinite spaces terrifies me." For me, on the contrary, after these times of election excitement, of newspaper polemics and all our wordy agitation, it has a message of consolation and encouragement. The universe knows how to accomplish its work without any noise; no declamations echo in those heights, no flaming programme obtrudes itself among the tranquil constellations. I believe that French society has at last entered upon that happy stage where everything is accomplished quietly and without any jars, because everything is accomplished in its full maturity. There will be reforms, great reforms even, but they will come to pass without having been given a name, and they will not trouble the calm life of the nation any more than the dropping of ripe fruit troubles the still autumn days. Humanity will raise itself insensibly toward fraternal justice, just as the earth that bears us rises with a silent motion in the starry spaces."

"My dear fellow, I can hardly wait to answer you, I have so many things to say."

"No, no; don't answer me to-night, only look and listen. While we are dreaming of the future and arguing, everything that lives, everything that exists is giving itself up to the joy of the passing moment, to the instant sweetness of the serene night. The peasants are going in groups to the meeting-place of the farm, to gather in the corn, and as they go they are singing in a full chorus; the awakened snake trembles a little and then sleeps again in the mystery of the thicket. In the stubble, in the dried-up fields, some poor little creatures are still singing; their music is not insistant and universal as it is in the warm spring nights or the hot summer nights; but they will sing to the end, as long as they are not really frozen by the winter. Fires of dry grass glow in the middle of the fields, and the moonlight envelops and softens their gleam; it is as though the spirit of the earth flamed and was mingled with the mysterious light of the skies. Stray dogs are barking at a belated waggon that comes slowly along the road, lit up by a lantern and drawn by a little donkey. A lovelorn owl hoots plaintively in the chesnut grove; the ripe chesnuts fall with a thud and roll down the little valleys. A small green frog is croaking near the fountain; the heavens shine and the earth sings. Come, let the universe be—it contains joy for all—it is Socialistic after its own fashion."